PICTURE FRAMES
In An
Afternoon

PICTURE FRAMES

In An
Afternoon

Kaye Evans

Sterling Publishing Co., Inc.
New York

PROLIFIC IMPRESSIONS PRODUCTION STAFF:

Editor: Mickey Baskett
Copy: Sylvia Carroll
Graphics: Dianne Miller, Karen Turpin
Photography: Greg Wright
Administration: Jim Baskett
Styling: Laney Crisp McClure

ACKNOWLEDGEMENTS

Kaye Evans thanks the following for their generous contributions:

Custom Frames:
Nurre Caxton
Sunrise, FL

Ready-Made Frames:
Intercraft, Inc.
Austin, TX

Matboards and Section Frames:
Nielsen & Bainbridge
Paramus, NJ
www.nielsen-bainbridge.com

Prints:
Geme Art, Inc.
Vancouver, WA 98660

10 9 8 7 6 5 4 3 2 1

Library of Congress Cataloging-in-Publication Data Available

Published by Sterling Publishing Company, Inc.
387 Park Avenue South, New York, N.Y. 10016
Produced by Prolific Impressions, Inc.
160 South Candler St., Decatur, GA 30030
©1999 by Prolific Impressions, Inc.
Distributed in Canada by Sterling Publishing
c/o Canadian Manda Group, One Atlantic Avenue, Suite 105
Toronto, Ontario, Canada M6K 3E7
Distributed in Great Britain and Europe by Cassell PLC
Wellington House, 125 Strand, London WC2R 0BB, England
Distributed in Australia by Capricorn Link (Australia) Pty. Ltd.
P.O. Box 6651, Baulkham Hills, Business Centre, NSW 2153 Australia
Printed in Hong Kong
All rights reserved
Sterling ISBN 0-8069-3947-8

TABLE OF CONTENTS

Kaye Evans
Contributing Writer

Kaye Evans, CPF

Kaye Evans, CPF, has been a professional picture framer for over 20 years, owning and operating her own Ace Hardware and K's Korner Frames for over 14 of those years. She has been an international educator in the framing industry for many years, and has to her accomplishment over 9 videos on different aspects of picture framing technology. Her most recent one was on Framing Needleart. Add to this number the many printed publications on the art of picture framing and you will realize the talent in Kaye's teaching ability. Additionally she is regular contributor for *Picture Framing Magazine*, a publication for the framing industry.

For many years she has been an Educational Consultant for Nielsen & Bainbridge, carrying their message about Alphamat Artcare to the masses. Additionally Kaye works with other manufacturers to bring the professional tools and materials in the industry to the highest standards possible. She has worked tirelessly with the Professional Picture Framers Association on the recertification committee for Certified Picture Framers. She was among the first to become a certified instructor for this Re-Certification Program.

"Aspiring to be among the top educators in the Professional Picture Framing Industry may not seem to be all that grand, but it is my accomplished dream. I am a framing educator who travels to the "ends of the earth" to carry the message about the importance of Preservation Framing Practices to the framing retailers around the world.

My work on this publication regarding the correct methods for picture framing has been an important step to help bridge the gap between the professional framer and the serious amateur framer. You are an important person to the custom framer. You should have choices. One is to be able to purchase the portions of the framing package you will need to accomplish the framing yourself. Should you decide not to frame it yourself you can help the professional framer design the artwork and let him or her create a safe preservation package for you. Which ever you decide, you are on your way to an exciting reference book that will be a source of information for years to come. Whenever you feel you have forgotten something you need only think about what you want to do and then refer to the section for that application.

Always remember if you have a valuable piece of art, whether it be monetary value, historical value, or sentimental value, to take it to your professional picture framer and insist on a preservation framing package. If you are simply framing for home décor or for the "FUN" of it, the most important thing you should do is to keep a great frame of mind!"

Sincerely,

Kaye Evans, CPF

Kaye Evans, CPF

Decorated Frames By:
Allison Stilwell, Patty Cox, Kathi Malarchuk, Marie Le Fevre

Learn the Ins and Outs of Professional Framing Plus Make and Decorate Your Own Special Frames

We frame pieces of art not only to hold them for display and to protect them, but to actually *showcase* them — to enhance their own beauty. In home decor today, it is important to know many ways to change and recreate new looks as easily as changing bed linens. Picture framing is on every wall in your home and is an important part of home decor.

This book covers both the technicalities and the artistic choices of framing. Every facet of framing is covered in Part I of this book. Then in Part II, you will find 33 frame designs to make yourself — either readily available frames decorated in a variety of ways or designs where the frame itself is actually made with cardboard or matboard.

In Part I of the book you will learn to measure your art and measure for your mat(s) and frame. You will learn to design creative mats and frames by your choices of mouldings and of mat colors and styles. You will also learn to cut standard mats and more elaborate mat styles. You will learn easy ways to mount your art, to join frames, and to finish the back in a dust-proof manner. This book will show you how to use the professional tools available to you at do-it-yourself frame shops. We do recommend that you use the tools there at the frame shop with their helpful advice and expertise rather than trying to purchase lesser quality tools of your own. We also do *not* recommend cutting your own moulding. It must be done professionally to fit properly at corners. But you can exercise your creativity in your choice of mouldings or by using pre-cut frame lengths available in a variety of styles. Additionally, you can learn to work with a Certified Picture Framer, if you prefer. You will discover how to ask the right questions and learn to know whether you are getting the best materials for your more valuable works of art.

In Part II of the book, learn to decorate pre-made frames as well as make your own frames from corrugated cardboard (which you would never guess is the frame material to look at the finished frame). Learn to cover them with handmade paper or wallpaper or even embossed tin from a soda can. Learn painting techniques, including faux finishes such as tortoiseshell, marble, or crackled painted wood. A variety of ways to gild a frame with a silver, gold, or bronze finish is also included here. The mixed media frames in this book range from beaded frames to mosaic tile frames to frames that are made dimensional with a variety of items, even flattened silverware.

So whether you wish to frame a treasured piece of art or have fun decorating or making frames for all purposes, learn how from this book. Get started now.

PART I
FRAMING WITH PROFESSIONAL RESULTS

By Kaye Evans, CPF

CAN I DO MY OWN FRAMING?

This is an important question. The answer is "YES you can!" When you don't know where to start, the task seems difficult. But if the steps are broken down into easy-to-understand sections, it becomes much easier. This book is not only educational, but will continue to be a reference book as your creativity grows. Education is easier if the path to it is organized. Following is the order of steps used to accomplish the framing of your art.

- **Designing** always comes first. The look and color of the framed art on the wall is critical to a creative home, so the aspects of good design should be developed first.
- **Measuring** is essential to the success of the project. Knowing how to identify 1/8" on a ruler is mandatory for a well-designed piece of art.
- **Tools and Supplies** to frame the picture is the next information with which to familiarize yourself. You can find professional tools at a do-it-yourself frame shop, available for your use. This book will teach you how to use them. These shops as well as other places also have the supplies you will need. Although you can purchase your own professional tools, using them at a framing shop is an economical option when you are framing only a few pieces.
- **Creative Matting** gives the framed art a look unique to the scheme of the room. Remember, the only way to get good at mat creativity is to practice!
- **Mouldings — Chops and Joined:** It is no longer necessary or desirable to cut picture frame moulding at the consumer level. Any professional framer can offer unjoined frames cut to custom sizes. In addition, they can join it and give it to the amateur framer. There are other ways to acquire mouldings that will be explored.
- **Glass Cutting** is one of the more cautious tasks in picture framing. The tools are important and a safe technique is even more important.
- **Mounting Techniques:** The artwork must be suspended within the frame to look as if it has no visible mounting techniques. This is easily accomplished with the proper materials and a good overview of the correct way to accomplish it.
- **Fitting and Finishing** of the artwork is the last step and one of the most important. It is possible to do a great job all along the way and have the frame package look poor because bad techniques were used to fit-and-finish the frame.

  With the information in this book to organize the task for you and teach you the techniques, you will surely conclude that *yes, you can* frame your own artwork. ❑

Pictured on page 9: This lovely eagle print is simply yet effectively framed, and it is easy enough for a beginner to accomplish. We will use this example to show you start-to-finish how simple framing can be. The 8" x 10" print is framed in a 12" x 14" wood frame. The stained wood that allows the woodgrain to show enhances the rustic nature of the scene. The art is double matted with two colors. The light grey top mat picks up the main color of the print and has the result of expanding its size. This mat is 2-1/4" wide. The navy blue liner mat defines the print itself and enhances the contrast of values within the print. The mats were cut with a simple bevel cut. ❑

DESIGN ESSENTIALS

There really *is* a place to start when creating the mat and frame for your art. That place is color. With simple information, the design elements of art become much easier. Start by understanding some design guidelines. The eye should travel inward toward the art, and the overall feeling of the finished piece should be one of complete satisfaction. The print used on this page is titled "Eagle", created by *Geme Art.* This image can have a quiet look of elegance and detail by starting with some basic thoughts.

Choosing Your Mat & Frame

Find the dominant color:

Turn the image upside down (Photo #1). Notice which color jumps out to take attention. This will probably be the focus mat and frame color. Using the color wheel, locate the color that will be closest to this one. This will be the dark blue/violet. (Photo #2). Because the focus mat is traditionally strong in color, it is probably best when used as the bottom mat. The color of the top mat should be light and soft in feel. The only exception is when the print is very dark. In this case the dark mat would need to be reversed and used on the top and the light mat on the bottom.

Find the complementary colors:

Work with the complementary color harmony to create a great design every time. Look at a color wheel. Notice that the colors which lay directly across from each other are friendly and complement each other (Photo #3). Examples: Yellow and Violet — a symbol of Eastertime; Red and Green — for a festive Christmas feel. Every color has a complement and it sits directly across the wheel. The eye must see these two colors to get the satisfaction of the design. If both colors are not present, the physical eye will continue to move around to locate it. If not found by the physical eye, the mind's eye will invent the missing color once the eyes are closed. Photo #4 shows the color wheel with two complementary colors emphasized. The dominant color in this print was a blue/violet of the background. This will be our liner mat. The complementary color (across color wheel) is a beige which is in the Yellow/orange family. Use the color wheel to select good color combinations.

Remember to contrast the colors. Use a tint with a tone or a tint with a shade. Never use two tints, two tones, or two shades together. One will get lost by the other from a distance.

Choose the mat colors:

Photo #5 shows a display that you may find in a framing shop to help you select your mat colors. Select the closest color of mat to the colors you determined on the color wheel. Most art looks best when doublematted. So you will choose your focus color for the bottom mat and complementary color for the top mat.

To make sure the color is correct both in harmony and in balance, try first putting the liner mat on top and then putting it on the bottom. Does the picture look heavy with the liner mat on the top? After putting it on the bottom, did the image appear to lighten not only in color but in feel? If so, the combination probably works.

Don't make a final decision about the mat colors and textures until the frame moulding is placed around the matting to give you a total presentation!

Choose the mat width:

The top mat should be nice and wide. This will emphasize the art. Narrow mats only make the finished presentation look "cheap."

If the image is a long horizontal one, use a "weighted" mat (increase the size of the lower mat side by 3/4" to 1") to prevent the bottom portion of the design from looking skinny. If a vertical image needs to have an appearance of height, simply make the sides and top of the mats slightly more narrow than the bottom.

Choose the mat style:

Remember that creative mat cutting can give the eye a path upon which to travel inward toward the art and give the look of great design. Adding an offset or V-groove mat can give the presentation more interest than just a simple double mat. A double mat gives ten times more excitement to the image than a single mat.

Select the frame moulding:

The moulding should echo the style of the image. A nature print looks best with a natural frame such as a stained wood frame. A formal painting would need a more formal frame such as an ornate gold leafed frame. An art photo would look great with a sleek metal frame. Glass should enhance the image and not detract with reflection. Not all art will need glass such as an oil painting.

View the entire presentation:

Place the mats and frame moulding together to see if it gives the proper effect. (Photo #6) The most effective way to view it would be to place the entire design on the floor against a gray background and walk around it. View it through one eye only, then through both eyes. Does it satisfy your feeling of elegance and pride? If so, move on to cutting the mats and assembling the frame, then on to finishing. ❑

Photo #1. Turn the image upside down. Notice which color jumps out to attention.

Photo #2. Using the color wheel, locate the color closest to this one for the focus mat.

Photo #3. Pick a contrasting, complementary color for the other (usually the top) mat.

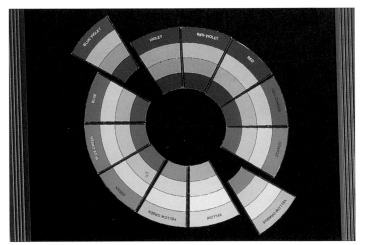

Photo #4. Color wheel with complementary colors selected.

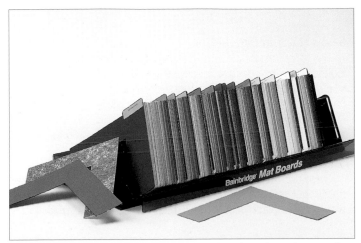

Photo #5. Choose samples of the mat colors from the selection of samples in the framing shop.

Photo #6. Place both mats and the moulding at the edge of the image to see the total effect.

Understanding the Color Wheel

There are three Primary Colors. There are three Secondary Colors. There are six Intermediate Colors. All of these combine to make a color wheel. White is the essence of all color and black is the absence of all color. Grey is the magic mixture of these two powers and is *the* color that allows every color to look like itself. When trying to make a color decision, use a grey background to assess them. Afterimage is the need to see both colors in a complementary harmony. The Artist color Wheel gives all the information on proper color harmonies.

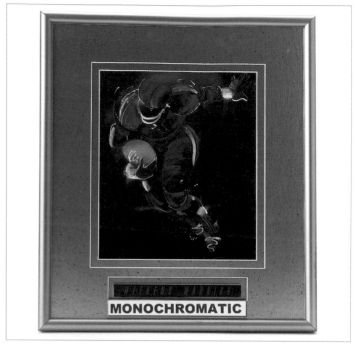

Monochromatic: The use of any shade, tint, or tone of one color

Complementary Harmony: The combination of a shade, tint, or tone of one color and crossing over the wheel to choose the opposite color. Example: blue and orange.

Split Complements: The choice of one color with the second color being on one side or the other of the complement color across the color wheel.

Triad: Color scheme that has three colors equally spaced from each other on the color wheel. Example: the three primary colors — red, blue, and yellow.

Analogous: Combination of shades, tints, or tones of colors that are next to each other on the color wheel.

Achromatic: A colorless scheme using blacks, whites, and greys.

Designing With Color

- Light colors move forward and dark colors recede. Used thoughtfully, you can create a feeling of depth.
- The colder the color, the smaller the amount of that color needed to achieve balance.
- The colors on one side of the color wheel (from yellow-green to violet) are cool colors and can be used to "cool off" the feeling of a print.
- Use both warm and cool colors to provide contrast.
- If two colors of the same tint, tone, or shade are used, the eye will not be able to separate them and the effect will be wasted. A non-color can be used to divide the color and will help both be seen.
- The human eye likes to see a greater proportion of cool colors than warm.
- Use an accent or third most predominant color and it will focus and move the eye.
- Gray is a neutral. Use it in a dark shade of your main color to add richness.
- If you use one color in great quantity and then look away and close your eyes, you will see the complement of this color.
- Color theory can be learned as well as felt! ❏

MEASURING ESSENTIALS

There are two different types of design to consider in the measuring process. There is first the Open Design. This is an image that looks better if there is open space surrounding the design area. This is the measuring method shown in Photos #1 and #2. The second type of design is the Closed Design. This is used when the image looks more attractive if the mats or frame cover a smaller amount of the image and do not allow any blank area to be exposed (Photos #3 and #4). Both types of designs are easy, but it is necessary to decide which is to be used before the final measurements are decided.

Determine the Size of Mat & Frame

Measuring is critical to the success of the project. Learn to use a ruler accurately. Look at 1" on a ruler, divide it in half and notice the 1/2" mark. Divide the half inch again to create 1/4" and again to create 1/8". Most measurements do not go below 1/8" as the allowance in a frame will accommodate this small amount. Once a good understanding of the tape measure is accomplished, the correct measurements will be an easier task. A good quality cloth tape measure is the best tool because it is long, lightweight, and will not harm art if dropped upon it. It is not necessary to stretch it to get the measurement.

How To Measure

1. Place the image on a flat work surface.
2. Using a cloth measuring tape, measure the desired viewing area of the image both vertically and horizontally (Photo #1). Normally this is the printed area. In the case of needleart it is from the edge of the outside stitch on one side to the edge of the outside stitch on the other side. This is the first measurement or the **Design Area.**
3. The next step is to determine how much space should show between the design and the inner edge of the mat (or the frame in case a mat is not being used). In prints, it is usually the area of white between the picture and the matting. Universally this is 1/4" to 1" on the top and sides and 1/4" to 3" on the bottom. This open area can vary with each image to give the best visual appeal. This becomes the **Open Area.** (Photo #2)
4. When both the design area and the open area are combined, they create the total amount of image that is viewed in the opening of the mat (or the frame, if a mat is not used). These two measurements added together will create the **Inside Dimension.** This is represented by E and B on the Fig. 1 diagram.
5. The matting (optional) is the next measurement needed. This area can vary to give space and balance. Traditionally in the framing industry, the standard rule of thumb is 3" on each side of the mat. But remember, thumbs bend and so should some rules. Wider looks much better than too narrow. The

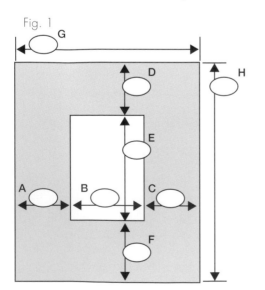

Fig. 1

Measuring Examples

Final Measurements for an Open Design

Design Area	8" x 10"
+ Open Area	$^1/_4$" x $^1/_4$"
= Inside Dimension	8 $^1/_2$" x 10 $^1/_2$"
+ Mat Area (both sides)	1 $^3/_4$" x 1 $^3/_4$"
= FRAME SIZE	12" x 14"

Final Measurements for a Closed Design

Design Area	8" x 10"
- Open Area	$^1/_4$" x $^1/_4$"
= Inside Dimension	7 $^1/_2$" x 9 $^1/_2$"
+ Mat Area (both sides)	2 $^1/_4$" x 2 $^1/_4$"
= FRAME SIZE	12" x 14"

average consumer tends to request a narrow mat simply because it seems less expensive. A "weighted" mat (larger on the bottom) will make the framed presentation appear to be better proportioned. The horizontal mat measurement is represented by A and C in Fig. 1 and the vertical measurement is represented by D and F.

6. Add A, B, and C together to determine the horizontal frame size. The result is G on the Fig. 1 diagram.

7. Add D, E, and F together to determine the vertical frame

size. The result is H on the Fig. 1 diagram.

8. These totals (G and H) are the frame size and should be the size of the frame to order.

Formula for calculating frame size for a matted image:
- Design Area + Open Area on both sides = Inside Dimension
- A (mat width) + B (inside dimension) + C (mat width) = G (horizontal frame measurement.
- D (mat width) + E (inside dimension) + F (mat width) = H (vertical frame measurement.

Open Design (With *area around art showing*)

Photo #1. With image on flat surface, position tape measure at very edge of the design. Measure total design area from edge to edge in both vertical and horizontal directions.

Photo #2. Add the desired amount of open space. If there is a signature on the bottom, add the open area and the signature area for the total open area on the bottom. Then add this measurement to the open area at the top of the image.

Closed Design

Photo #3. With image on flat surface, position tape measure 1/4" inside the edge of the printed image.

Photo #4. Measure up to 1/4" from opposite edge of image to obtain the measurement. Do this in both directions.

Supplies & Tools
Tools Used for Matting & Framing

Create a framing tool box that will organize and store the framing tools and supplies you keep at home. A good storage container is a large fishing tackle box with compartments small enough to hold the small tools and also deep enough to hold some of the larger tools.

The numbered photographs showing tools and supplies will help you know just what the proper name is for each tool or supply need. This will enable you to ask for them with confidence and recognize them easily when you encounter them at a do-it-yourself frame shop. Below are the definitions of tools which match the tools in the photographs. There are mat cutting tools, frame fitting tools, and glass cutting tools.

Professional Mat Cutter: Not shown. See it in the photo of cutting a mat in "Creative Matting" section. There are many mat cutters on the market. The best way to determine which one you need is to determine how much matting you will be doing. If you will be cutting more than four or five mats a week, it would be easier to get a more professional version. The cost of cutters varies. The more features on the machine, the more creativity it can accomplish. The less expensive models push instead of pull. The professional models pull, so look for one that pulls. If you do not wish to invest in a mat cutter, a quality mat cutter is available for your use at a do-it-yourself frame shop.

JT-21 Stapler (#1 in photo): The stapler is used to staple objects to mounting surface. Staple 1/4" or 5/8".

Small Padded Sanding Block (#2): The sanding block is used to perforate dust cover paper.

Craft Knife (#3): Needed many times when it is necessary to cut in very tight areas with a sharp blade. The knife will hold various sizes of blades. A very useful size blade is #11.

Utility Knife (#4): Used to trim, cut, and score various materials. It uses a #1991 or #1992 blade.

Clean Paint Brush (#5): Used to remove lint and dust from surfaces.

Sponge Brush (#6): Used to clean and remove lint and dust from glass and the surface of the art.

Needlenose Pliers (#7): Used to pull wire in the fitting and finishing process.

Tape Measure (#8): A cloth tape is preferred. It is used to determine size of frame.

Metal Ruler (#9): Used for trimming or to make a straight edge.

Decorative Scissors (#10): (Optional) In matting, this tool is used to create decorative paper edges on the matting.

Small Scissors (#11): Needed to cut thread in needleart mounting.

Fabric Scissors (#12): Necessary to cut fabrics for various projects. Sharp cutting scissors are essential.

Paper Scissors (#13): There are many needs for a pair of less valuable shears. These will be used to cut wire, polyester batting, and heavier material.

ATG Gun (#14): A tool used to apply double sided adhesive to attach mats together and place a layer of adhesive to the edge of a wood frame to hold dust cover paper. ❑

1

2

10

3

11

4

5

12

6

13

7

8

14

9

FAIRGATE   23-112   12" CENTER-FINDING RULE 12"

MADE IN U.S.A.
COLD SPRING, NEW YORK

17

More Tools Used for Matting & Framing

Hammer (#1 in photo): Used in hanging your finished framed art.

6-in-1 Screwdriver (#2): This will include two sizes of Phillips head driver as well as two sizes of slotted or straight driver. It also includes a 1/4" and a 3/8" nut driver.

Pro-Trim Knife (#3): Very useful for trimming dust cover paper.

Frame Master Point Driver (#4): A tool to insert nails into back of frame

Glass Breaking Pliers (#5): Tool used to break glass

Glass Cutters (#6,7): Tools designed to score glass for breaking. Steel Wheel (#6) or carbide (#7) tips are available; the latter is preferred.

Protractor (#8): A tool used to line off exact 90-degree corners; used in needleart or to square a matboard

Slip Joint Pliers (#9): Tool used in fitting and finishing the back of the frame.

Scratch Awl: (#10) This is a tapered tip tool designed to make holes. If the tip is heated, it can be bent at a 90-degree angle. This will produce a useful tool to attach screw eyes to the back of a wood frame.

Ice Pick (#11): A very sharp pointed tool designed for picking ice. It is very useful for making the holes in the frame back to secure the hardware.

Mounting Tool (#12): Used to burnish (rub) adhesive into the substrate

Burnishing Bone (#13): A tool made of animal bone used to smooth down paper hinges

Stiff Blade Putty Knife (#14): Used to push the Push Points or inserts into the frame

Hot Glue Gun (#15): For gluing objects to a mounting surface within the frame.

Bent Tweezers (not shown): (Optional) For handling tape ❏

1

2

3

4

5

6

7

8

9

10

11

12

13

14

15

19

Matting Supplies

Supplies are the consumable products used in framing. Keeping them organized will make them easier to locate when needed. There are many sources for framing supplies. The best way to find the needed supplies is to first start with the local frame shop that also carries other crafts. Explain to them what is needed and ask where the retail area is for these items. Sometimes they can be for sale but not be on the selling floor.

Matboard

A mat serves at least three purposes:
1) The first, and probably the most important, is to protect the artwork. The mat is placed over the artwork to hold it in place and to keep the glass from touching it.
2) The second purpose is to hide the mechanics of mounting and hinging the artwork.
3) It's third purpose is to cause the eye to travel from the corners of the frame to the center of the artwork. It should be quiet enough that the eye doesn't get caught on its busyness, yet bright enough to keep the eye moving inward.

Matboard is highly important to your framing project, therefore you must understand more about the materials themselves. The most valuable part of the frame package is the image or art. The matboards which house this image must be of a quality to take care of the artwork. There are several types of matboards available in the marketplace, and they are very different from each other.

Regular Paper Mats:

This is the standard type of board buffered to an alkaline pH. What does that mean? Simply put, it has calcium carbonate added to give the board buffers to hold in check the acids of the board itself. The buffering is strong when the product is new, but the board may change in quality as it ages. Because it is buffered, it is usually acid free when new. As the package ages, the buffering gets used up and the board cannot hold the acids in check. Then the board itself becomes a source of damage to the artwork. These boards come in many colors and also have the center or core of black. They are of the quality and creativity you need to frame short-lived projects which can easily be replaced and have no monetary value. Figure 1 shows the plies of this matboard.

White Core Boards:

For non-conservation framing jobs where unique and dramatic textures could really make a difference, the white core of the board maintains a great look. The core of the board will not discolor over time. It also contains a buffering pH but, like the standard board mentioned above, the buffering is leaned upon heavily and eventually used up. The board will someday begin to damage the art it was supposed to protect.

Alpha Cellulose Boards:

This is of the purest and highest quality cellulose fiber. Alpha cellulose can be derived from cotton or highly refined wood pulp. Cotton, in its raw state, is the purest form of natural cellulose. Cellulose is the chief constituent of all plants. Cellulose has three chemical forms: Alpha, Beta, and Gamma. The Alpha form of cellulose has the longest and therefore the most stable chemical chain, in turn creating the longest and strongest paper-making fibers.

Other Matting Supplies Pictured

Pre-cut Mats (#1 in photo): Mats that already have an opening. They are available in a number of sizes and colors.
Craft Sticks (#2): Used to rub down various adhesives
Weights (#3): For holding down the print during mounting. You can use items such as film cartridges filled with sand or washers.
T-Pins (#4): Used to punch holes in the mounting board to insert thread during lacing
Safety Blades (#5): Used for trimming mats.
Tapestry Needle & Silk Pins (#6): Use tapestry needles, sizes #16, #18, #20, #24, and #26, for mounting needleart. Silk pins are thin pins to hold needleart in place until it can be mounted.
Cotton Swabs (#7): For cleaning in tight areas of glass
Pencils (#8): Use a #2 pencil for sketching design and writing measurements. Use a #6-H pencil for marking measurements on the back of mats. Use red, blue, and orange pencils to mark lines on back of mats.
Latex Gloves (#9): Used to straighten needleart after lacing
Framer's Tape (#10): Used for hinging
ATG Tape (#11): Double-sided tape used in the ATG Tool
Foam Core Board (#12): For spacer mats

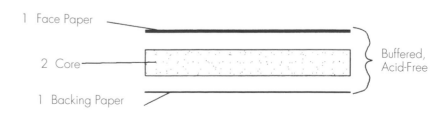

Fig. 1 – Matboard Understanding

1 Face Paper

2 Core

1 Backing Paper

Buffered, Acid-Free

Framing Supplies

You can see exactly what each supply is in the numbered photographs which match the definitions below.

Clear Glass (#1 in photo): Used in frame over artwork.

Non-glare Glass (#2): Used in frame over artwork.

UV Glass (#3): Used in frame over artwork.

Frame (#4): Moulding was chosen at a frame shop. Then the moulding was cut and joined by a professional framer.

Frames (#5,6): Ready-made frames

Metal Frame Pieces (#7): Two packages of two rails which will join to create size of frame. (Thumbnailed)

Wooden Frame Pieces (#8): chopped and thumbnailed frames from a professional framer

Compartmented Box (#9): For holding and organizing small framing supplies.

Glazing Points (#10): Used to put mounted artwork into frame

Strap Hangers (11): For creating a flat hanger for back of frame

Screw Eyes (#12): For wire hanging

Coffee Filters (#13): Used for wiping glass. Non-ammonia glass cleaner used for cleaning glass is not pictured.

Easel (#14): Allows frame to stand rather than hang

Wire (#15): Braided, used to hold the frame on wall ❏

GLASS
AND
BACKING
8x10
CLEAR GLASS
INCLUDES BACKING:
CUT OUT
CARDBOARD
TO MATCH
GLASS SIZE

CONNOISSEUR

Document Frame
Cadre pour Document
Marco para Documento

8½x11in / 22x28cm

CREATIVE MATTING
Styles of Mats

There are various styles of mats from simple to very fancy. Some are fancier than others. Some of the fancier styles can actually add value to the artwork. But remember, the overall design is important. Some pieces of artwork may actually look better with the simpler matting techniques.

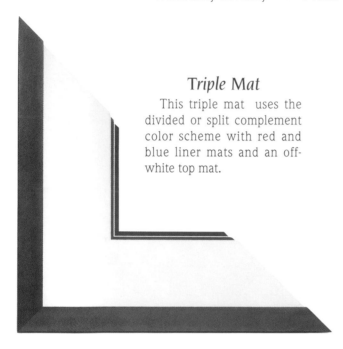

Triple Mat
This triple mat uses the divided or split complement color scheme with red and blue liner mats and an off-white top mat.

Triple Mat With Offset Corners
This mat style uses three matboards for a top mat and two liner mats. It is shown with offset corners in a monochromatic color scheme.

Double Mat
The double mat consists of a top mat and a contrasting bottom or liner mat. The double mat shown here is a very fancy variety, however. The top mat not only has a fillet edging added but is also V-grooved.

Stop V-Groove and Free-Hand Design
This type mat is done by professional framers. The "stop V-groove" is a V-groove that does not continue all the way around the mat. Here the V-groove stops before the corners and a free-hand cut design with colors added is cut in the corners. Designs such as this give added value to artwork.

Four-Layer Offset Mat

This four-layer mat is a combination of two double-mat sets. The bottom set features a contrasting liner. Both mats of the top set match the top mat of the lower set and feature fillets. It's a very elegant design.

Hand Carved Mat with Watercolor Panel

A watercolor panel of a *slightly* different shade is fitted along the inside of the mat. The mat is then intricately hand-carved near the corners.

Open V-Groove With Strips Added

This V-groove is widely separated and a V-grooved checkerboard strip of two other colors is added in the separation. The checkerboard colors are repeated for two liner mats. Colors are complementary.

Doubled-Matted Keystone Corner

The top mat features a V-groove mat that is widely spaced with a keystone corner cut. The bottom mat is a crackled texture mat with a simple bevel. Spacer mats are placed between top and bottom mats. **Spacer Mat(s)** are cut from foam core board, and used to hold the decorative mat(s) forward from the art and backboard, or between mats. ❏

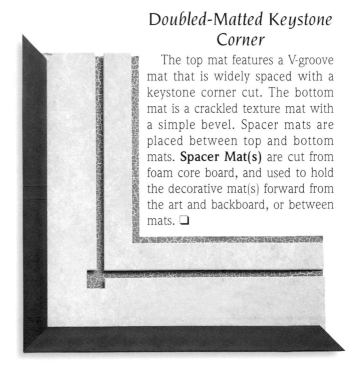

Cutting a Double Mat

The double mat is considered the bread and butter of the framing industry. When a mat is needed, the double mat should be the first consideration. It consists of a top mat and a contrasting bottom or liner mat. In paper borne art, the double mat is necessary to insure that the print will not rest against the glazing. In needleart, it maintains the *minimum* depth allowed to provide air space between the artwork and the glazing.

The inner edge of a mat has a beveled edge. (Even in the past when matting was cut with a simple mat knife and straight edge, it had a beveled edge.) Webster defines "bevel" as a slop-ing edge between two parallel surfaces. The fine sloped line created by the bevel causes the artwork to look more appealing. The bevel breaks the look between the mat and the artwork. This beveled edge can easily be different colors since today matting companies have created black centers (cores), white centers, and solid color centers

While cutting the double mat has been done in many ways, there is a specific way of cutting to cause the mats' two surfaces to look perfectly parallel. It is also faster than other methods. This method will be demonstrated here.

■ Step 1: *Cut Matboard to Fit Frame Rabbet*

Each mat must first be cut to the size of the frame rabbet (the notched section in the frame back — usually larger than the frame opening). Cut two blank pieces of matboard for double-matting. *Note: The blank or sized-to-fit matboard should have four perfect 90-degree corners. If this is not the case, every cut done past this point will be skewed and will be noticed immediately when the artwork is viewed.* Use the following steps to be sure the matboard is cut to fit.

1. Start with a blank larger than needed. Place it on a flat surface and measure from one edge and mark two points on the blank for the vertical cut. Place a metal ruler against the marks and cut the full length of the board. (Fig. 1)
2. Measure and mark two points for the horizontal cut and cut in the same manner. (Fig. 2)
3. Check to be sure it is squared by placing a protractor against the edge of the board to be sure the perpendicular side is 90-degrees. Then follow the steps below to cut the mat.

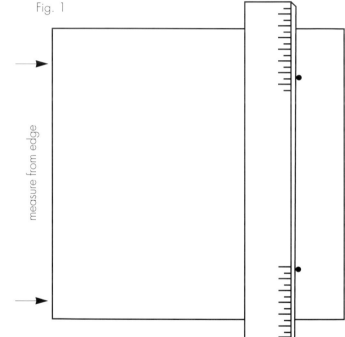

Fig. 1

measure from edge

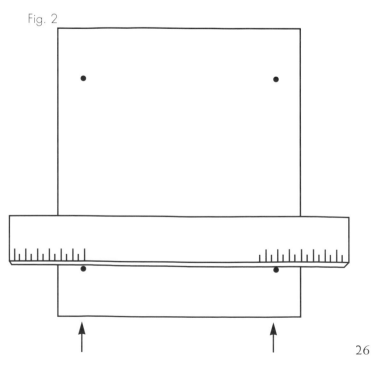

Fig. 2

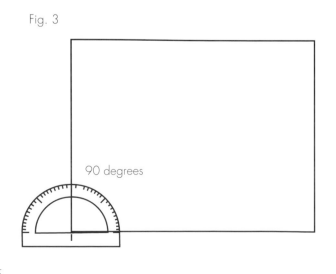

Fig. 3

90 degrees

Step 2: Measure and Mark Top Mat

1. Place a registration mark on the back of both blank mats as shown in Fig. 4 to insure that you know how to replace the fallout (center of the mat) into the opening correctly.

2. **Set the mat guide for the width of the mat.** We will be cutting a 2" wide mat. Place mat against the mat guide. This is the sliding bar of the mat cutter against which the matboard rests. It is on the left side of the cutter head. The cuts you will make here are the second most important angles after the perfect 90-degree corner on the mat blanks. **Check the accuracy of the mat guide.** Check this by setting the mat guide at 2" and placing a scrap piece of matboard against the guide at the bottom of the cutter. Insert the blade into the board at the midpoint and score the board from the midpoint to the edge. Lift the handlebar of the cutter and slide the blank up the cutter to the top section of the mat guide, (Important note: If your mat cutter has a top screw on the mat guide, it must be tightened to insure that the matboard will not slip.) Make a score the full length of the board. Gently bend the board at the cuts. Do they align perfectly over each other? If not, the mat guide is not square and it should be corrected immediately. The mat will be only as perfect as the mat cutter and the operator can make it.

3. **Note the width(s) and mark the cutting lines.** Write the recipe (the amount to cut) on the outside edge of the back of mat, using a fine pencil mark. A good marker is a 6-H pencil. Use a very light hand when marking. It is desirable to erase all pencil lines after the mat is completed, and the lighter the mark the easier it is to remove. Draw a line on each side at 2" as shown in Fig. 5 and Photo #1. Draw a line on each side at 2", making sure the corners intersect. If the borders are the same width, only the right side needs to be noted with the size.

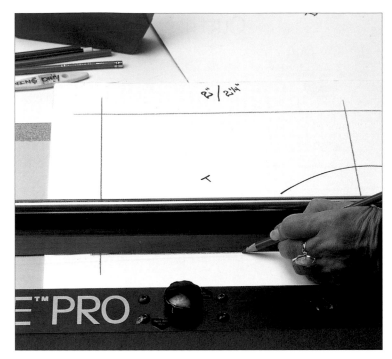

Photo #1. Measure and mark sides of mat opening.

Fig. 4

Fig. 5

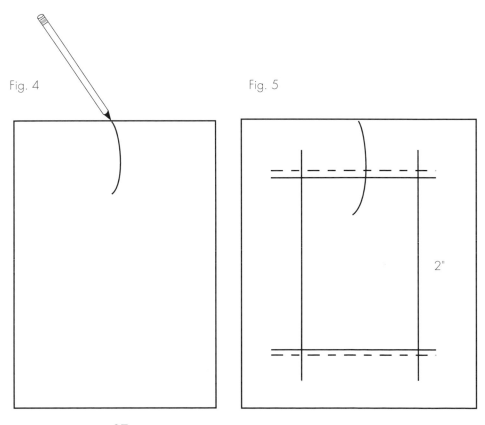

■ *Step 3: Cut the Top Mat*

1. **Cut along the lines.** After checking to insure that your blade is sharp, start the cut at the area pointed out in Fig. 6 and shown in Photo #2. The dotted line in this diagram represents the position of the blade as the cut is started. The cut is *not* started at the drawn line. Cut the top mat on all four sides.

2. Carefully remove the fallout and set it aside. This is shown in Fig. 7 and Photo #3.

Fig. 6

Start cut here.

End cut here.

Fig. 7

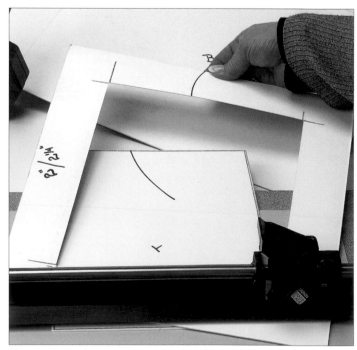

Fallout

Photo #2. Start the cut where shown (beyond the marked line).

Photo #3. The fallout is the area of matboard that is removed when all cuts are made.

Step 4: Prepare the Liner Blank

1. **Reduce size of liner mat blank.** Reduce the size of the bottom or liner blank by 1/4" on *only two* sides — one long and one short side. Place the liner mat blank under the cutter bar, face side down, and reduce with the bevel cutter. This will cause the blank to be reduced by approximately 1/8" on each side. It is important not to reduce this too much.

2. **Align the two matboards.** Place the top mat face down on the work surface. Place double sided adhesive tape along the opening of the mat (Fig. 8 and Photo #5).

continued on page 30

Fig. 8

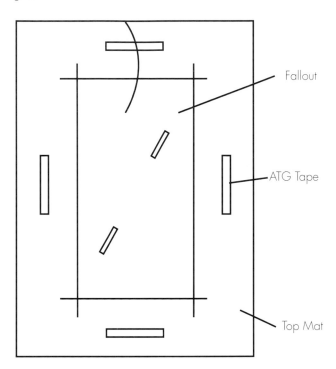

Fallout

ATG Tape

Top Mat

Photo #4. Reduce the size of the liner mat blank.

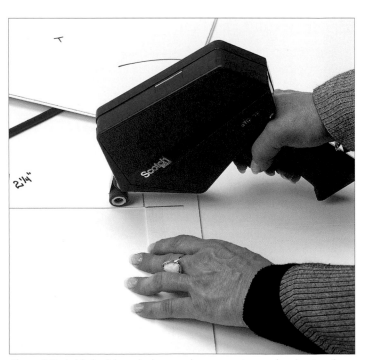

Photo #5. Add double sided tape along opening on backside of top mat.

Step 4: Prepare the Liner Blank

continued from page 29

3. Place the liner mat face side down and centered over the top mat (Fig. 9 and Photo #6). *Make sure that none of the liner mat extends out over the edge of the top mat in any location.*

4. Turn the double mat to the front side, noting on which end the register marks are located. Align the register marks to perfectly reposition the fallout (Photo #7).

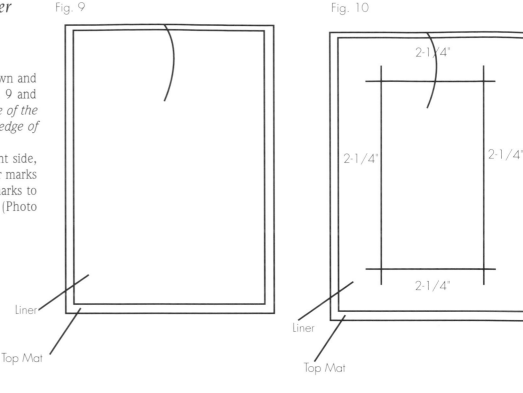

Fig. 9 — Liner / Top Mat

Fig. 10 — 2-1/4" / 2-1/4" / 2-1/4" / 2-1/4" / Liner / Top Mat

Step 5: Cut Liner Mat

1. Remove the slip sheet from the mat cutter for this step. Your top mat will serve the function of the slip sheet. Change the guide bar setting to 2-1/4".

2. Place the set of mats into the mat cutter, face down. Mark the four sides of the mat with a 6-H pencil on the backside.

3. Make the cuts, starting inside marked lines where an imaginary dotted line would be. (See Fig. 10 and Photo #8.) Watch closely for overcuts.

4. Lift the mat from mat cutter (Photo #9).

5. If the fallout does not come out immediately, carefully turn the mat to the front and place on a flat surface. Place one hand on the front of the fallout and slide the fingers of your other hand between the two surfaces to release the double sided adhesive tape. This will release the fallout from the top mat and will allow you to get into the corner of the liner mat with a sharp blade to free the corner. Trim where necessary (Photo #10). *Be careful not to change the angle of the bevel with the blade as you cut!* You will have a perfectly parallel double mat. ❏

Photo #6. Center liner mat black over top mat.

Photo #7. Reposition the fallout of top mat.

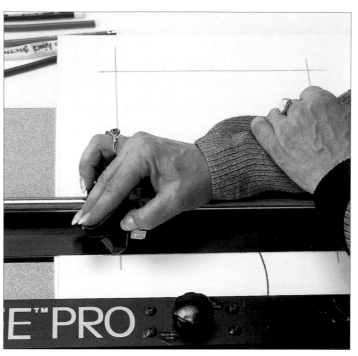

Photo #8. Cut the liner mat.

Photo #9. Lift mat from mat cutter.

Photo #10. Trim hung-up corner(s), if needed, with craft knife.

This pansy watercolor painting has a double mat of two soft but contrasting colors to match the softness of the painting. The light blue-violet liner mat picks up the blue-violet from the painting. The top mat is the soft beige of the painting's background. The beveled edges of the two mats have been rubbed with a metallic gold wax to echo the elegant gold carved frame.

The double mat surrounding this painting of fish is brown (liner mat) and a dull green (top mat), picking up the shades of the fish and the water. They are also nature colors used for a nature painting. The core of these matboards is a soft gold-beige color, moderating between the colors of the painting and the gold of the faux tortoiseshell narrow frame. The narrowness of the frame maintains the simplicity of the subject, while its finish adds just a touch of elegance.

Cutting an Offset Corner Mat

Once the double mat is accomplished, the sky is the limit as to what can be created in matting. In all cases, it is important not to overpower the image with the matting. However, a simple and quiet creative corner will add greatly to the beauty of the finished presentation. With this technique, small corners are created in the corners of the mat. Though it looks extremely difficult to execute, you will be successful with the offset mat by following the step-by-step process and repeating the instructions exactly as given.

◼ Step 1: *Measure and Mark Mat*

1. Have available a red and a blue pencil. Determine the size you want your corner to be — 1/4", 1/2", 3/4", or 1". Corners smaller than 1/4" do not work well. Add the width of the mat border and the size of the corner to get the width to mark your matboard blank as shown in Fig. 2. Below are two common sizes:
   - 8" x 10" frame with border of 2-1/4" + offset 1/2" = 2-3/4"
   - 11" x 14" frame with border of 2-3/4" + offset 3/4" = 3-1/2"
2. **Mark larger measurement.** Set the mat guide at the *largest* amount — the total of your width and corner measurements. In the example shown in Fig. 1 this is 2-3/4". Mark all four sides with one color of pencil. DO NOT CUT YET.
3. **Mark smaller measurement.** Set the mat guide at the smaller number — the mat width without the corner — in this case 2-1/4". Mark all four sides with the second color of pencil.
4. **Color in the offset corner** and mark with X's where corners start. See Fig. 2 and Photo #1.

◼ Step 2: *Cut Mat*

1. **Cut first color lines.** When the clamp of the mat cutter is placed over the board, the marked X becomes an arrow (Photo #2). With the mat guide set at the smaller number — in this case 2-1/4" — cut from the arrow, following same

color lines, on all four sides. The fallout will be bound with undercuts. (Fig. 3) This is normal.

2. **Cut second color lines.** Reset mat guide to the larger number — in this case 2-3/4". Cut from arrow to arrow, following second color lines (Fig. 4). Remove and discard fallout (Photo #3).

Fig. 1
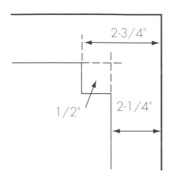

Fig. 2
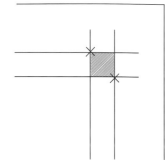

Fig. 3
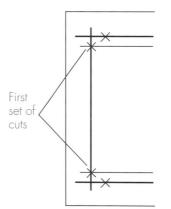

First set of cuts

Fig. 4
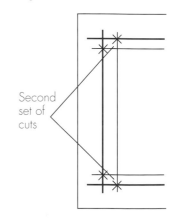

Second set of cuts

Photo #1. Color in corners.

Photo #2. When covered with clamp, the X becomes an arrow. Start at arrow.

Photo #3. Remove fallout

The photo of the framed memorabilia from an ancestor shows a triple mat with offset corners. The top mat is also V-grooved and a spacer mat is used behind the decorative mats to add more depth for the dimensional items that are framed. The top mat and bottom liner mat are beige with a crackled finish — an aged look to add to the theme of oldness. The navy blue liner mat adds the contrast needed for definition. To complete the presentation, an antique gold frame is used, continuing the theme of age plus adding a touch of honor.

Cutting a V-Groove Mat

This is a creative mat that adds not only quiet elegance but includes the look of design lines. The V-groove appears extremely difficult to accomplish, but really is easy if the exact instructions are followed. Always cut the V-groove first (on the top mat, if more than one mat is used). Cut the V-groove closer to the opening than to the outside edge of the mat. Use a new blade for each set of four cuts. This will insure crispness to the look.

A V-groove mat is shown in the photo of framed memorabilia on previous page. The crackled texture top mat has been cut with a V-groove.

Step 1: *Measure and Mark Mat*

1. Determine the position for the V-groove. A good rule of thumb is to place the V-groove closer to the opening of the mat than the outside edge. Below are two common sizes of mats with V-groove positions indicated:
   • 8" x 10" frame, V-groove at 2", Opening at 2-1/4"
   • 11" x 14" frame, V-groove at 2-1/2", Opening at 2-3/4"
Always mark and cut the V-groove prior to cutting the mat opening.
2. Set the mat guide at 2" for an 8" x 10" mat or 2-1/2" for an 11" x 14" mat.
3. Mark all four sides. *Don't forget to make the register mark on the backside.*

Step 2: *Cut the Mat*

1. Start the mat cutting with a fresh blade, essential for a V-groove.
2. Cut at the V-groove markings.
3. Carefully remove and *retain* the fallout. Set the mat aside for later use.

Step 3: *Cut the Fallout*

1. Set the guide bar for a V-groove according to the instructions given for the mat cutter being used. Place a fresh slip sheet into the cutter against the guide bar. Place the fallout against the mat guide with the color side facing you. Place a scrap mat at the leading edge of the fallout (Photo #1) to get the blade tracking smoothly before the blade touches the corner of the fallout board.
2. SLOWLY cut all four sides of the fallout. Fig. 1 shows how you will be creating a beveled edge to the fallout in the opposite direction from the one made when the first set of cuts were made. Be sure to turn the scrap mat above the cut each time you turn the fallout.

Step 4: *Replace Fallout*

1. Place #810 tape onto short sides of mat back. Extend it into the opening only 1/8". Burnish the tape into the back of the mat.
2. Place the cut mat face up on your work surface. Refer to registration line to insure correct placement. Position the fallout back into the opening of the mat, aligning registration marks (Photo #2). The tape will catch the fallout and hold it in position, yet allow it to be repositioned.

Photo #1. Recut edges of the fallout.

Photo #2. Replace fallout, aligning registration marks.

■ Step 5: Cut Mat Opening

1. Change the mat guide to the measurement for the opening
   — 2-1/4" for an 8" x 10" mat or 2-3/4" for an 11" x 14"
   mat.
2. Mark and cut the opening, cutting on inside lines (Photo
   #5). Fig. 2 shows an end view of the resulting V-groove cut
   and Photo #6 shows the finished V-grooved mat.

Fig. 1 — End View of Fallout
Cut on dotted lines to create V-groove.

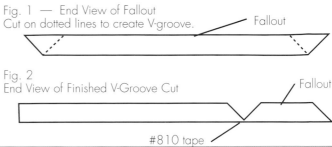

Fig. 2
End View of Finished V-Groove Cut

Photo #3. Add tape to long sides on back.

Photo #4. Burnish tape with bone burnisher.

Photo #5. Cut mat opening.

Photo #6. Finished V-grooved mat.

Cutting a Cove Mat

A cove mat gives depth so that you can frame dimensional items such as antique memorabilia. A cove mat can be used as a backboard to mount dimensional items. If this is done then an opening is not cut. It can also be used to hold the glass away from the mat that is cut with an opening.

■ Step 1: Measure and Mark Matboard

To create a mat with a 1-3/4" cove, measure and mark the mat on the mat cutter at the 1/2" position. Be sure to extend the lines to the *exact* edge of the matboard. Refer to Fig. 1.

■ Step 2: Cut Opening

Cut out the opening at the 3" measurement. (If the mat will be used to mount memorabilia, omit the dotted line cut at the 3" position.)

■ Step 3: Score Mat.

Use the fallout to gauge the depth of the mat cutter blade. Raise the depth of the blade in the mat cutter so that it will cut approximately two-thirds of the way, *not all the way,* through the board. *Score* along the 2-1/2" lines. See Fig. 2. Remove mat from the cutter and place on a flat surface.

■ Step 4: Cut Pie Wedges in Corners

1. The cut you just made will intersect in the four corners. This is where you will be cutting the pie wedges to create the depth of the cove. Use a utility knife and a straight edge. Hold the knife as straight and upright as possible. A bevel angle will not work on these corners. Cut from the exact intersection of the 2-1/2" mark. This will create a pie shaped wedge that you will remove.
2. Gently bend the sides of the mat downward to create the sides of the cove mat. Pull the first corner together and tape with a strong acid-free tape such as Framer's Tape II.

Photo #1. Items to assemble.

Photo #2. Cut decorative edge of paper with decorative edging scissors.

Fig. 1

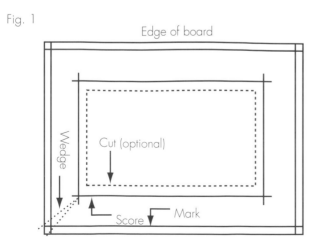

Edge of board

Wedge

Cut (optional)

Score   Mark

Fig. 2

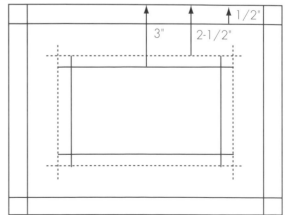

1/2"
3"   2-1/2"

Antique Memories — Framed Memorabilia

Both the elegance and the oldness of yesteryear are captured with this mat and frame. The mat is the same green marbleized texture as the backboard. The shaped paper edge gives the feel of delicate lace. The carved frame is gold, heavily antiqued with umber.

1. Cut an offset mat with a 1-1/2" border.
2. Using decorative scissors, cut art paper strip 3/4" wide with one straight edge and one decorative edge (Photo #2). Apply ATG tape along the edge of the opening on back of mat.
3. Turn the mat to face side. Carefully apply the decorative paper strips along all four sides of opening so that the decorative edge of the strips extends into the opening of the mat.
4. Sew all pieces of memorabilia to the backboard, using buttons on the backside of the backboard to secure them.
5. Cut photo mount board smaller than the old photo and hinge to the backing board. Use glue to attach. Glue photo to mount board.

MOUNTING ART & PHOTOS

How To Mount With Hinges

Hinges are pieces of tape used to attach the artwork or photo to the mat. Use framer's tape as it is an acid-free archival pressure-sensitive tape. *Hint for Beginners: Before hinging "real" artwork, practice on pieces of typewriter paper.*

▢ Step 1: *Hinge the Mat to the Backboard*

1. Place mat face down on surface.
2. Place the backboard face up, with top of backboard butting up against top of mat.
3. Place a strip of framer's tape on backside of mat across top edge of mat and extending beyond mat onto backboard. (Photo #1). Burnish tape to mat and to backboard.
4. Now the mat can fold down into position over backboard. Both will be face up and the hinge will be hidden.

continued on page 42

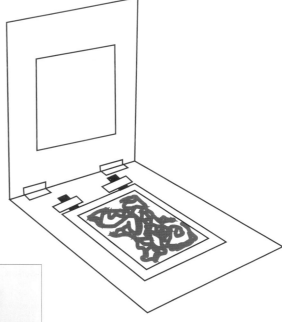

Fig. 1. Art mounted with a T-hinge.

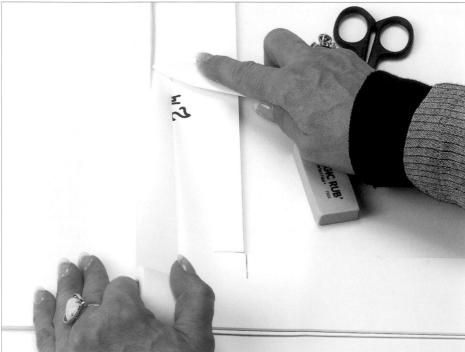

Photo #1. Attach hinge to mat.

Pictured right: The framed rustic photograph is enhanced by a double mat with gold fillets at the edge of the top mat. The mats were planned to support the photo and not overpower it. The narrow gold mat just inside the frame is a metal frame liner. The dark green liner mat picks up the shadow areas of the photo. The top mat is a sueded mat, adding texture. The narrow gold frame completes the presentation, but the effect is that of a wider frame because of the frame liner.

continued from page 40

▉ *Step 2*: *Hinge Art*

1. Slip art into position between mat and backboard. An eraser is a big help in positioning the art. (Photo #2). This will also help to avoid fingerprints on the art.

2. When art is in the desired position, hold it in place with weights.

3. Lift the mat and mark on the backboard where corners of art are positioned.

4. Remove art from backboard. Place the art face down on a clean surface. Determine the number of hinges needed and their placement.

Photo #2. Move art into position with an eraser.

Photo #3 Holding art in place with weights, lift mat and mark correct position on backboard.

Photo #4. Apply hinges to art.

continued from page 42

5. Place a piece of tape, about 1" long, onto top back of art, perpendicular to top edge. Position tape so that about 3/4 of the tape extends beyond the top edge. (Photo #4).

6. With mat lifted, replace the art in position on the backboard, aligning with the corner marks made on backboard.

7. Place another piece of tape over the sticky side of each hinge (Photo #5).

8. Fold matboard back down over the art.

Photo #5. Place art on backboard. Place another piece of tape across each hinge.

How to Create a Free-Floating Mount

Here is a charming option for mounting photos, watercolors, or other types of art.

▇ Step 1: *Deckle the Edges*

Tear the edges of the photograph by holding the photo close to tearing edge and pulling forward with your other hand (Photo #1).

▇ Step 2: Mount Photo

1. **Use dry adhesive paper on back of photo,** as follows. Pull off release paper and place dry adhesive paper on back of photo. Place release paper on top of photo and burnish across photo (Photo #2). Pull off backing paper. This will leave a covering of adhesive on back of photo.
2. Place photo in position on mounting board (Photo #3).

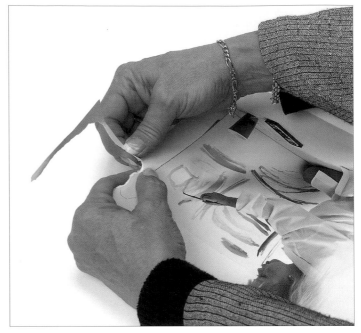
Photo #1. Tear to deckle edges of photo.

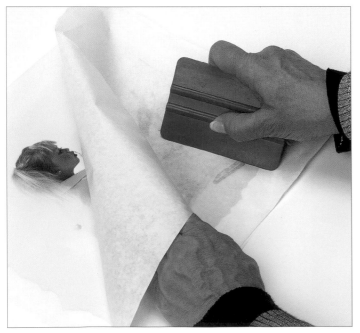
Photo #2. Place release paper on top of photo and burnish.

Photo #3. Place photo on mat mounting board.

No mat is used in this framing presentation. The deckled photo is mounted on a navy blue matboard, which is then mounted on a decorative beige backboard. Spacers are used on back of the mounted photo to hold it forward in the frame. The backboard is then framed with a navy blue frame with gold edge. The navy blue repeats the navy blue of the matboard holding the photo and the narrow gold edge adds just the right accent.

45

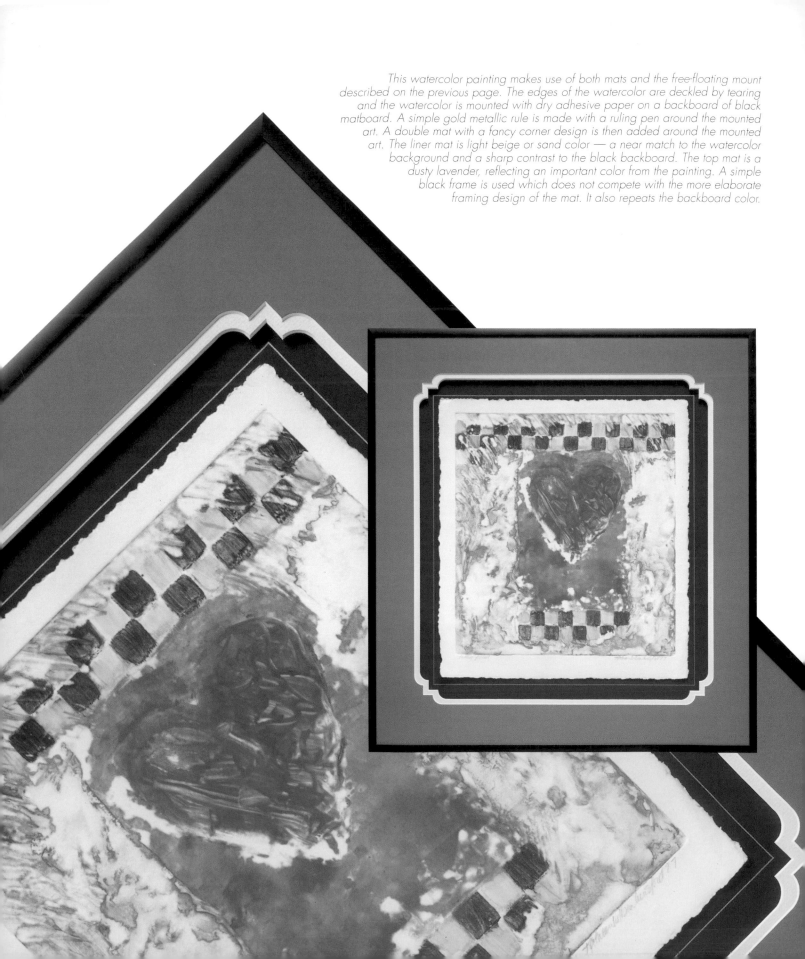

This watercolor painting makes use of both mats and the free-floating mount described on the previous page. The edges of the watercolor are deckled by tearing and the watercolor is mounted with dry adhesive paper on a backboard of black matboard. A simple gold metallic rule is made with a ruling pen around the mounted art. A double mat with a fancy corner design is then added around the mounted art. The liner mat is light beige or sand color — a near match to the watercolor background and a sharp contrast to the black backboard. The top mat is a dusty lavender, reflecting an important color from the painting. A simple black frame is used which does not compete with the more elaborate framing design of the mat. It also repeats the backboard color.

This collection of photos uses one large top mat and two liner mats with five openings for the photos. In addition, the top mat has a cutout decorative design at top and bottom which exposes the color of the middle mat, and the cut design reminds us of the Southwest where the photos were taken. The photos are hinged in place behind each opening. The liner mats are of the two main colors in the photos — the colors of vivid land and sky. The top tan mat is a lighter shade of the brown liner mat. This display is framed with a brown wood frame with narrow antique gold inner edging.

CREATIVE FRAMING
Types of Frames to Choose

There are a number of ways you can acquire a frame for your art. If it is a standard size, you may choose from a number of ready-made frames on the market. If it is not a standard size or if you want a particular look that you cannot find, there are two options. You may choose from a wide selection of frame mouldings at a frame shop and have a professional order the rails and/or framer make the frame for you. Or you may find the type mouldings you want in ready-cut unjoined frame strips, called "sectional frames." These come two to a package so that you can buy one package for the width you need and another for the length you need. These are cut so that they will fit together properly and the hardware for joining the frame strips comes with the package.

About Frame Moulding — Chops & Joined

Moulding is the material that is joined to create a frame. By looking at Fig. 1, you will see a profile of the moulding. The most talked about part of the profile from a fitting and finishing position is the rabbet. The rabbet (not misspelled) of a frame must be deep enough to accommodate all the materials needed to support and accent the image. The lip of the moulding actually supports all the materials housed within the package. The spine or back of the moulding serves to support. It traditionally stays flat because it and the bottom of the frame are the two positions that must rest securely against the cutting equipment to insure an accurate cut.

Mouldings are manufactured in various methods. Wood mouldings come in blanks. These are pieces of wood that are then moulded or cut with several rotating knives to create all sides of the profile at the same time. In the case of metal, the profile is actually extruded from a billet of aluminum and is pushed through a template that produces metal mouldings. Fig. 2 shows the profile of a metal frame. The manufacturer of all types of moulding have become very advanced at cutting and finishing with various materials to produce a rich, hand-rubbed, furniture finish quality — not only for wood but metal and polymer, as well.

Types of Moulding

The types are wood, metal, polymer, and a new material to the marketplace called MDF. MDF consists of small wood particles which are mixed with a glue and compressed under high pressure to produce a solid wood-like appearance.

Hardwoods are, of course, the oldest types of moulding. They have been used for centuries to surround and support the image and framing materials. For years hardwood has been the support and beauty for the framed artwork. However, unknown to the masses, the wood frame has also been the source of damage to the artwork. The wood frame (as well as others) can do damage to artwork because it contains acid and chemical materials. Trees are held together by a substance called lignin and this is very acidic. Therefore all wood frames should be sealed to prevent the acid in the wood moulding from damaging the artwork.

There is only one type moulding that is truly safe for the image. That is metal. It has been determined from testing that metal needs no sealer to be housed next to the image. It is "inert" and will do nothing to harm the artwork.

Wood must be sealed by applying a paint sealer several times to the rabbet or applying a polyester tape to the rabbet. This will help prevent the lignin from damaging the artwork housed within the frame.

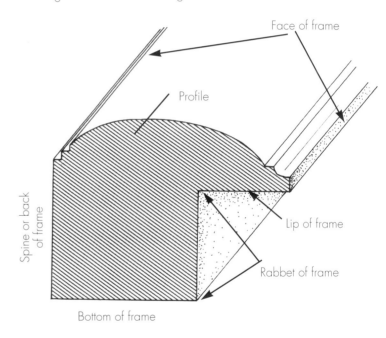

Fig. 1 – Profile of Moulding

Face of frame

Profile

Spine or back of frame

Lip of frame

Rabbet of frame

Bottom of frame

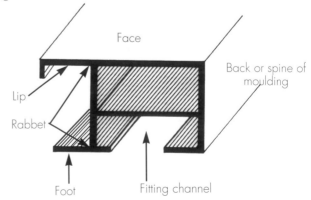

Fig. 2 – Profile of a Metal Frame

Face

Back or spine of moulding

Lip

Rabbet

Foot

Fitting channel

Wood and metal will hold much more weight than polymers. But no thin mouldings will support a sizable piece of art. Remember to stay with the wider profiles of moulding. A good rule of thumb is to use 1/2" to 3/4" of moulding width for framed art under 16" x 20". Profiles of 1" to 1-3/4" will usually support a size up to 24" x 36". For sizes larger than this, only profiles of 2" wide or more are used to support the image and other materials — the matting, backboard, and glass. The profile of the frame sometimes determines how much weight it can support, but the major factor is the overall width.

The profiles shown in Fig. 3 will help to identify the various looks mouldings can possess.

Can I buy moulding from a building supply store and use it for picture frames?

In a word, no. There are several reasons why the profiles made for framing are unique. First is the rabbet. Wood moldings used in home building do not have the rabbet to hold the "sandwich" of the art. Secondly, the moulding used for picture framing is dried to a lower moisture content to insure that it does not split or warp on the wall. The wood itself is a much higher grade of lumber than that which is traditionally used in home building. FAS (First and Select) wood is used to hold the quality of the moulding at a high standard.

The desire to cut moulding yourself may be strong, but please resist it. The saws or choppers used to cut picture frame moulding are of extremely accurate quality. The blades must be carbide tipped and especially controlled to cut a baby-smooth surface for the mitre of the moulding. The teeth to accomplish this must be above 80 and are usually 90 and above. The cost of just the blade to cut this quality is well over $100.00 and the saw to run this type of blade is usually around $2,000.00 and above. There is another cutting machine called a chopper. It works as the word indicates. It uses very sharp chisel point blades to bite or chop the mitre and accomplish the cut in several bites.

Cutting picture frame moulding on an inexpensive saw can never give the kind of cut that will insure a good mitre. In many cases, even professional picture framers no longer cut their own. In cases of hard-to-cut or very expensive mouldings, even they leave it to experts better than themselves.

The second machine mentioned is where the word "Chop" originated. The chop is the project of cutting the lengths of moulding needed to complete a frame to the desired size, such as 8-1/2" x 13-3/4". This is ordered and delivered quickly for the frame to be joined and the more difficult parts of the framed piece to be completed.

Custom Joined Moulding

The consumer can enjoy this service by working with the professional framer. Let the framer know that the reason for purchase is not to try to get a cheaper price, but to have the fun of fitting and finishing the artwork yourself. Once a rapport is reached with the framer, the custom joined frame will be ordered for the amateur. When it arrives it will be assembled by the framer and purchased as a joined frame.

The great advantage of this type of purchase is that the professional framer probably has a machine called an underpinner. This is an automatic nailer that shoots a v-shaped nail into the bottom of the frame and, with the additional use of vinyl wood glue, secures the mitres of the frame. It is the best and strongest of the various methods of joining.

Photo #1: a custom joined frame.

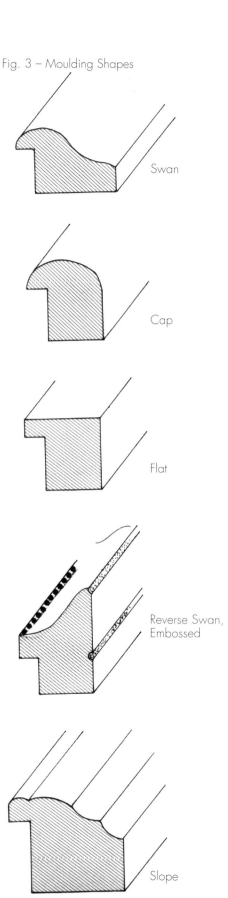

Fig. 3 – Moulding Shapes

Swan

Cap

Flat

Reverse Swan, Embossed

Slope

Ready-Made Frames

The easiest type of frame to purchase is the ready-made. These are frames already cut and joined that come in "standard sizes." Two such frames are shown in Photo #2. The popularity of this type frame is easily understood when you consider the volume of ready-made frames sold. Consumers use millions of ready-made frames each year. The backing and glass is usually part of the package. It is an easy task to simply pick up a frame and start the fitting and finishing process.

Within this category there is a section called "Photo Frames." These are the small frames that house an easel that allows the frame to be free-standing.

Photo #2. Ready-Made Frames

Sectional Frames

These are one-half of a frame in a prepackaged display that contains the materials needed to assemble one-half of a frame. These frame strips are better referred to as "rails." Both the rails and a joined frame made from them are shown in Photo #3. The good thing about this type of purchase is the versatility of the sizes. The frame dimensions can each be increased by 1" increments by purchasing longer rails. These can make almost any size as you buy the rails for the width and the length separately. The limitations are the small variety of available finishes and widths of mouldings available.

These frames are usually wood or metal. If they are wood, the method of joining is traditionally thumbnnailing (explained in another section). If the sectional frame is metal, the method of joining is to insert metal hardware into the channel at the back of the frame and pull and lock the corners together.

Photo #3. Sectional Frame

Custom Chops

It is possible to work with your local professional framer to buy what is referred to as a "chop." This is ordered cut-to-size by the customer. The chops are shown in Photo #4. The method of joining this frame is by thumbnailing, or it is joined on a hand vise. Be sure to give the framer ample time to order and receive the frame, and let him know if the frame needs to be thumbnailed.

Remember, ordering in this manner puts the burden of assembly, and also the burden of mistakes, on the customer's shoulders. If the frame becomes damaged, it is unlikely that the framer will take back the chop. Accuracy is important. Just as a custom shirt is built-to-size, a custom chop is built to fit only the project for which it was purchased.

The advantage of this type of frame is the wide selection from the framer's wall. The sky is the limit for the type of frame that can be purchased.

Photo #4. Custom Chop

Joining a Custom Chop Frame

Thumbnailing is a joining system that is accomplished by routering out a small portion of wood on both sides of the mitre of the moulding. The shape of the routering is in either an "I" beam or "L" configuration. The frame is then assembled using wood glue and a plastic wedge sometimes called an insert. This method of joining is used when straight nails or v-nails are not an option.

Vinyl wood glue is used to hold the frame together permanently and the thumbnail holds the frame tightly together until the glue dries. The frame will have a more finished appearance if you use a colored wood stain to "dress" or hide the edge of the exposed corner prior to assembly. Take care not to get oil based stain on the mitre. If you do the glue may not hold the frame together. After joining, allow the frame to dry. Use nail hole filler in the joined mitre to "dress" the miter and insure that the seam of the joint will look professionally done.

Follow the step-by-step procedure below.

■ Step 1: *Prepare the Frame Pieces and Supplies*

1. Lay out all pieces and tools as shown in Photo #5. Place the frame on the work surface with the rabbet edge facing upward. The finish will rest on the work surface. Be careful that the frame is not scratched by debris on the work surface. Note the numbering in Fig. 4 of each rail of the moulding.
2. Place the matching rails opposite each other as shown in the diagram. Place the appropriate number of inserts next to each corner to have them ready when needed.
3. Place a quarter-size dollop of glue onto a small scrap of matboard approximately 4" x 4". It is important for the glue to lose some of its water content to gain a faster and better bond to the wood. This will help accelerate the drying time as the frame is being joined. (NOTE: When the glue skins over, it is probably too dry to use.)

continued on next page

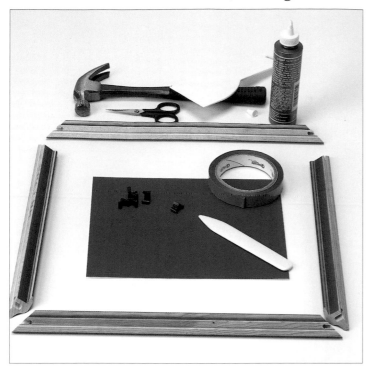

Photo #5. Lay out frame pieces and supplies.

Photo #6. Spread glue on one side of the mitre.

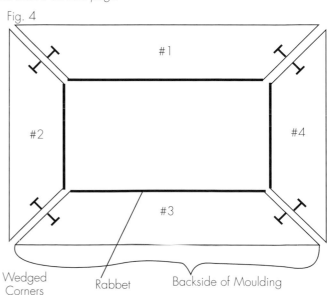

Fig. 4

#1

#2

#4

#3

Wedged Corners   Rabbet   Backside of Moulding

Joining a Custom Frame
continued from page 51

▪ *Step 2: Join Frame Pieces*

NOTE: If the profile of the moulding cannot lay flat, it will be necessary to support the frame in such a manner that the corner of the moulding will not rock. This is easily accomplished with a stack of scrap 4" x 4" matboards. Their thickness is perfect to build the necessary height needed to support the outside or inside edge of an unlevel profile.

1. The first corner to be joined will be rail #1 to rail #2 (Fig. 5). Spread the glue evenly over the surface of *one* side of the mitre, not both (Photo #6). Pull the corner together with a tight appearance. Look at the insert to insure that the correct *rounded* end will be inserted into the routered opening of the mitre.

2. Hold the insert between your fingers and swipe it through the dollop of glue so that some glue will be carried by the insert into the bottom of the opening. This will also make it easier to push in the insert. Do *not* fill the opening of the mitre with glue. This will make the job of joining more difficult.

3. Push the insert into the opening, being careful to keep it straight (Photo #7). Push with your thumb until the insert is fully seated in the opening. If the insert cannot be placed into the opening with a little resistance, a stiff surface must be placed between the insert and your thumb. A stiff bladed putty knife or one of the 4" squares of scrap matboard may be placed over the top of the insert to help make the insertion easier. Push the insert into the opening until flush with the back of the moulding. Position a common or flat screwdriver on the insert and push to be sure it has gone into the opening completely.

4. **Join next corner.** Join rail #2 to rail #3 in the same manner (Fig. 6). Move the frame around quickly in order to assemble it before any glue dries.

5. **Join last rail.** Place glue on both mitres of rail #4. Swipe the inserts through the glue and insert each into the openings of rail #4 (Fig. 7). Place rail #4 over the top of the joined three-sided frame and firmly seat both inserts simultaneously (Fig. 8 and Photo #8). Using the stack of 4" x 4" scrap matboards will make this task easier.

6. **Examine and realign where needed.**As a final step, carefully examine the frame from the front side and align the corners as perfectly as possible while the glue is still wet (Fig. 9). You have only approximately five minutes before the glue begins to set, so work efficiently.

7. **Tape over rabbet.** Place Mylar tape over the rabbet of the frame to prevent the acid in the wood from damaging the art (Photo #9).

Photo #7. Push insert into opening.

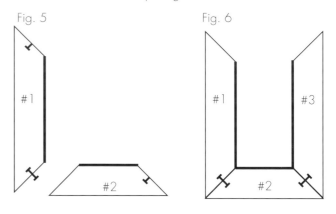

Fig. 5   Fig. 6

Fig. 7

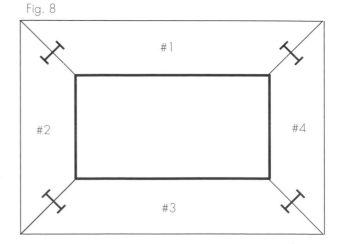

Fig. 8

Photo #8. Seat both inserts of rail #4 simultaneously.

Photo #9. Place Mylar tape over rabbet of frame.

Fig. 9

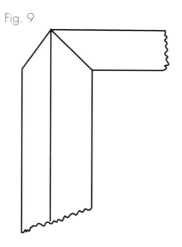

Tips For Joining Wood Rails

- Don't try out the insert for size, then remove it. This is a "one time fit." If the insert is inserted and then removed, it will greatly affect the fit.
- Avoid hammering the insert into the opening. Pressing firmly will achieve a much better bond and tighter corner. As a *last* resort hammering may be an option, but do it only with a rubber mallet.
- Avoid wiping the mitre of the frame with a damp cloth to clean off excess glue. This will only weaken the bond. To make this task easier, purchase a fingernail brush from a hardware store. This should not damage even the softest of finishes.
- If the frame has two thumbnails per corner, place the shorter thumbnail first, then the longer one. ❑

Joining a Metal Frame

Even though the metal frame is considered to be the easiest of all frames to assemble, it can become a nightmare if certain guidelines are not followed. The following step-by-step instructions will make putting together a metal frame a snap.

1. Be sure the working surface is flat. Open the package and lay out the frame, choosing top, bottom, and side rails. The top will be the furthest distance from the edge of your work surface, the side rails will be perpendicular to the edge of the work surface, and the bottom rail will be closest to the edge of the work surface. Open poly bag of hardware.

2. There are eight angle plates — four with screws and four plain. Combine one plain and one screwed angle plate to make the first corner's set of plates. Slide the two plates as one unit into the corner of rail #1 and corner of rail #2. Slightly tighten, just enough to keep the hardware from falling out of the corner.

3. Using the same technique, slide another set of corner plates into the corner of rail #2 and rail #3. Slightly tighten.

4. The last step created a "U" shape. Slide the glass, mat picture, mounting, and backing into the channel. Check for lint or dust in the package.

5. Insert the remaining corner angles into each end of rail #4. Slide the exposed angles into the "U" shaped rails and tighten all screws in all corners. It may be necessary to adjust screws to be sure that the corners are flush with each other.

6. Put the Omni Hangers into each of the side rails approximately one-fourth of the distance down from the top of frame. Tighten the screw in each. Insert braided wire into the holes in the Omni Hanger and tighten with the technique given in the section on fitting.

7. Add bumpons to the bottom corners of the frame. ❑

FITTING & FINISHING

The word *fitted* may seem strange to you, but it is the term that professional framers use to refer to the closing of the frame. When you spend time carefully constructing your mats and frame and adding your artwork you want to make sure it is fitted and finished correctly. Fig. 1 shows a cutaway of a typical frame.

It is important that the frame hold the entire "sandwich". A deep rabbet on the frame itself is important. If the artwork sticks out the back, the frame will not hang on the wall properly.

A good choice for the dust cover (the paper that protects the artwork on the very back of the frame) is giftwrap paper. Avoid wrapping paper that is folded; you will see the crease marks in back of the frame. Select a simple paper with rather muted colors that is not very shiny. (Shiny paper will not handle well as you apply it to the back of the frame.) Handle it carefully so as not to crinkle it. You may also select brown paper.

A final item needed on the back of the frame is the bumpon. This small, rubber-like sticky pad keeps the artwork space off the wall so air can get behind the picture, preventing mildew. It also protects the wall from the sharp edges of the frame. Lastly, it is placed onto the frame right after the dust cover is applied to identify the bottom of the frame.

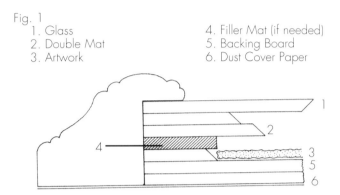

Fig. 1
1. Glass
2. Double Mat
3. Artwork
4. Filler Mat (if needed)
5. Backing Board
6. Dust Cover Paper

You will need some simple tools to complete the fitting process:
1. Glass cutter
2. Glass breaking pliers
3. Ice pick
4. White glue
5. Fine sandpaper
6. Wooden sanding block
7. Needlenose pliers
8. Bumpons

Cutting and Adding Glass

After the glass is selected, you will need to cut it to size. Select a glass cutter that has a carbide tip versus a steel wheel. This will make a huge difference when you actually score the glass. Find this at your local hardware.

Clean the glass with a good grade non-ammonia glass cleaner before you cut it. A good cleaning cloth is a coffee filter. Simply spray the cleaner on the filter and wipe the filter over the glass.

Wear safety goggles while cutting and breaking the glass.

▪ Step 1: *Score the Glass*

1. Dip the tip of the cutter in oil before each cut. This will make light work of the task. (Some glass cutters hold oil in the handle and it is dispensed automatically when cutting.) Never cut glass dry, as this will tend to chip out the score line and create shards of glass.
2. Hold the cutter properly as shown in Fig. 2. The angle of the cutter head is critical to a good cut. The small wheel should be kept perfectly upright to the glass.
3. Hold a straight edge on the glass and pull the glass cutter quickly down the edge of it to produce a good, clean line (Photo #1). Cutting the glass will produce a fine score line that should almost be hard to see.

Continued on next page

Fig. 2
How to hold the glass cutter

Glass Surface

Fig. 3
Line of score

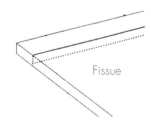

Fissue

A glass cutter does not actually cut glass all the way through. It creates a minute fissue through the glass.

Step 2: Break the Glass

To break glass cleanly, hold glass close to score line on one side of score line and, with pliers, bend downward on other side of score line. (Photo #2)

Step 3: Seam the glass

After cutting the glass, you will want to seam it to prevent the sharp glass from rubbing the frame and creating fine sawdust. Do this by simply running a whetstone once lightly over the edges of the glass. A whetstone can be obtained from the hardware store.

Photo #1. Using a straight edge and glass cutter, score glass.

Photo #2. Break glass on score line using pliers.

Fitting & Finishing the Frame

Step 1: Place the "Package" in the Frame

1. Place the matted artwork on a clean work surface with the art facing you.
2. Clean the glass once more.
3. Hold the glass approximately 2" over the artwork and drop it onto the artwork. This will force the last little dust fuzzies off the artwork.
4. Now place the cleaned frame over the glassed artwork (Photo #3).

Step 2: Secure the "Package" in Frame

1. Carefully flip the entire frame and artwork over to finish the fitting process.
2. Secure the artwork in the frame by pushing in either framer's points (Photo #4) or glazing points (Photo #5) into the rabbet. A point driver will fire these into place.

continued on next page

Photo #3. Place glass over matted artwork, then place frame over the glassed artwork.

Photo #4. Option 1: Push in framer's points.

continued from page 55

■ Step 3: Apply Dust Cover

1. Dampen the wooden edge of the frame with a slightly damp cloth. This will allow the glue to be applied more easily and the paper will adhere better. Remember that the less water that comes into contact with the artwork the better, so be cautious here.

2. Apply glue around entire area on back of frame. You may do this with an ATG gun which applies tape adhesive (Photo #6) or apply a tiny bead of white glue from the bottle and then spread it with a damp sponge (Fig. 5 and Photo #7).

3. Place an oversized piece of dust paper over the frame and slightly stretch the paper to press it into the glue (Photo #8). If the paper wrinkles, you have too much glue.

4. Trim the paper along edge of frame with a tool called a pro-trim knife (Photo #9). There is a second option which can be used to trim the paper — simply place fine sandpaper over a block of wood and rub the block lightly over the exact edge of the frame (Photo #10). This will perforate the paper and allow it to be easily torn off the back. You should notice a clean and smooth edge to the paper.

■ Step 4: Apply Bumpons

Attach them to the bottom back of the frame. One in the lower right corner and one in the lower left corner will be just right.

Fig. 4

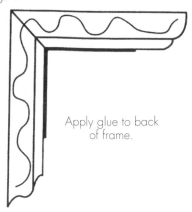

Apply glue to back of frame.

Photo #5. Option 2: Push in glazing points.

Photo #6. Option 1: Apply tape adhesive to back of frame with an ATG gun.

Photo #7. Option 2: Squeeze a tiny bead of glue around frame and spread it with a damp sponge.

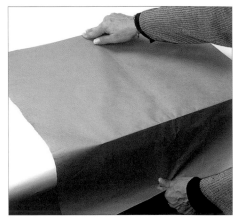

Photo #8. Press oversized dust paper over frame and press into glue.

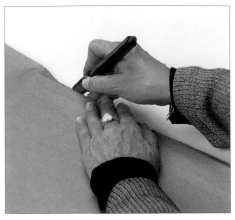

Photo #9. Option 1: Trim excess paper with a pro-trim knife.

Photo #10. Option 2: While glue is wet, sand lightly on exact edge of frame to perforate paper. Tear off excess paper.

Attaching Hanging Hardware

You will need to select the proper hardware to hang the artwork. The size of this hardware is important. You will place a screw eye into each side of the frame to hold the wire and the size is important. You will need a short-shank screw eye versus a long-shank (Fig. 4). (You might accidentally twist the long shank through the frame and out the front.) A good size for a 12" x 16" frame or smaller is a #213-1/2. Your local hardware store will show you the proper size screw eye.

The size of the wire is also important and the type of wire is critical. Wire will be twisted, braided, or simply pulled. The twisted and pulled wire will not hold the picture without stretching, so choose braided wire. A number 4 wire will hold up to 85 pounds on the wall — a good selection for the average frame.

Step 1: Attach Screw Eyes

1. The screw eyes should be positioned one-fourth of the distance down the frame. Measure the back of the frame on vertical sides. Using an ice pick, pierce a small hole into the side of the frame on each side. These will be starter holes for the screw eyes.
2. Slowly twist the screw eye into the frame so it will not break off (Photo #11). Stop the screw eye when it is tilted slightly inward so the wire will lean off the opening of the screw eye. A second option is to use strap hangers instead of screw eyes (Photo #12).

Step 2: Attach Wire

1. A hangman's noose, shown in Fig. 6, is a good example of a good wrap of wire. Stretch the wire across the back of the frame and make sure that the hanger can be attached to the wall and not show (Fig. 7 and Photo #14). Use a good solid hanger that is sized to the correct weight of the picture.

Fig. 5

 Short shank Long shank

Fig. 6

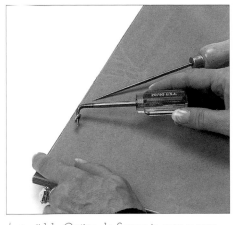

hoto #11. Option 1: Screw in screw eyes one-fourth of the distance down the frame.

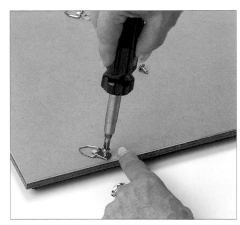

Photo #12. Option 2: Screw in strap hangers instead of screw eyes.

Fig. 7

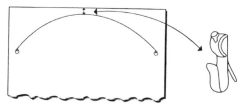

Photo #13. Attach wire to screw eyes or strap hangers.

Photo #14. Stretch wire across back and make sure hanger can be attached to the wall and now show.

PART II

MAKING & DECORATING
NOVELTY FRAMES

There is almost no end to the materials you can use for making frames,
and the ways to decorate them is limited only by your imagination.
In the following pages, you will learn to make your own frames from
cardboard, foam core board, mat board, even the aluminum from soft
drink cans. And you'll discover many, many ways to decorate both
ready-made and your handmade frames. There are painted frames and
personalized frames, frames made with wire and tin, frames gilded with
a variety of metallic products, decoupaged frames, frames decorated
with handmade paper, and "mixed media" frames which use almost
everything — from beads to old silverware.
These frames are inexpensive, and most are quickly made. This makes
them perfect for gifts as well as for yourself. There's a frame here for
every photo need.

PAINTED FRAMES

A little paint can turn a plain frame into a decorator item. Whether it's stripes on a plain wood frame or exquisite faux tortoiseshell or marble created on mat board frames, marvelous things can be done with paint.

Most of the frames here use easy craft acrylic paint. The faux tortoiseshell frame combines this type paint with liquid leaf paint and glass stain paint.

Crackle medium with acrylic paint creates yet another interesting painted effect. Simply paint on top of it and the topcoat cracks like weathered painted wood.

Supplies & Tools For Painted Frames

Craft Acrylic Paint

This is the quickest and easiest way to decorate a painted frame. There are many brands and hundreds of premixed colors. These paints dry quickly and cleanup is simple with soap and water.

Gold Liquid Leaf Paint

This is a brilliant metallic paint that resembles real gold leaf but is simply brushed on. Clean up with mineral spirits.

Glass Paints

These are transparent paints generally used on glass for a glass stained look. Here they are used on gold basecoated mat board frame for the faux tortoiseshell finish. The transparency allows the metallic gold basecoat to add depth to the appearance. These are applied directly from the applicator tip of the bottle. Clean up with soap and water.

Brushes

Basecoating or painting stripes is easily done with a sponge brush or a large flat brush. For the simple decorative designs, use a small round or liner brush. For one project, an old scruffy brush is used for stippling.

Tape

Stripes are quickly painted with crisp edges by masking off areas between stripes with masking tape or transparent tape. Paint remaining areas. Remove tape, and there are your stripes — straight and clean.

Cellulose Sponge & Feather

These special tools are used for marbleizing. To create the mottled colors of marble, various paint colors are dabbed onto the basecoat with a sponge. For best effects, tear off bits of the sponge on one side, especially along the edges so no straight lines will appear as you dab on the paint.

The irregular veins of marble are painted on with the tip and side of a feather. A turkey feather is a good choice. You can also buy "marbleizing feathers" at craft shops.

Crackle Medium

A product is used to create the cracked appearance of weathered paint. Apply it between an acrylic basecoat and topcoat to cause the topcoat to crackle, allowing the basecoat to show through the cracks. This is a popular instant aging process.

Sandpaper

Sandpaper is not only used to prepare the raw wood of a frame. It is also used here to sand down the painted surface to give an old, worn look. For wood frames, you will need sandpaper in various grits to prepare your wood and in medium grit to create the aged effect.

Finishes

There are a variety of finishes you can apply to your completed painted frame. When you don't wish to change the painted appearance, simply use **matte acrylic spray sealer.** For more gloss, use **waterbase satin varnish.** The faux tortoiseshell frame uses a **resin finish.** This special finish, for which two ingredients must be mixed together right before use, gives a thick and glassy finish that adds to the look of expensive tortoiseshell. ❑

Pictured right: Stripes in Neutral frame and Magical Stripes frame. Instructions follow.

Stripes in Neutral
Designed by Allison Stilwell
Pictured on page 61

■ Materials

Acrylic Craft Paint:
Gray
Ivory

Frame:
Wood rectangular frame with rounded corners, 11-1/4" x 12-3/4" x 3/4" thick with 3" x 5" opening

Other Supplies:
1" foam or flat brush
Transparent tape
Matte spray water base varnish
Sandpaper: fine, medium, and coarse grits
Pencil and ruler

■ Instructions

1. Sand rough spots and wipe with a tack cloth.
2. Basecoat with ivory. Let dry. Sand until smooth.
3. With a pencil and ruler, lightly mark every 1-1/2" across frame parallel to the 11-1/4" sides.
4. Mask off every other stripe with transparent tape. Paint the exposed stripes with gray. Let dry. Remove tape.
5. When thoroughly dry, sand with different grades of sandpaper to give the frame a well worn look. Sand until you achieve the look you want. Sand more around the edges and opening. Sand away some of the paint down to the bare wood.
6. Finish with several coats of matte varnish. ❑

Magical Stripes
Designed by Allison Stilwell
Pictured on page 61

■ Materials

Acrylic Craft Paint:
Ivory
Light aqua
Light mustard
Metallic gold

Frame:
Wood rectangular frame with rounded corners, 11-1/4" x 12-3/4" x 3/4" thick with 6-3/4" x 4-3/4" opening

Other Supplies:
1" foam or flat brush
Small round or liner brush
Masking tape, 2" wide
Chalk
Matte spray water base varnish
Medium grit sandpaper
Pencil and ruler
White eraser

■ Instructions

1. Sand rough spots and wipe with tack cloth.
2. Basecoat with ivory. Let dry. Sand until smooth.
3. Carefully align 2" tape from corner to opposite corner so that stripes will be diagonal. Keep center of tape even with corners of frame. With pencil and ruler, lightly mark every 2" diagonally on each side of tape. Mask off every other stripe with the 2" tape.
4. Paint exposed stripes with light aqua diluted with a bit of water. Let dry. Remove tape.
5. Trace patterns for designs onto tracing paper. Retrace lines on backside of traced patterns with chalk or pencil. Place in position on frame and retrace each design with a pencil or pen to transfer designs to frame. Refer to photo of project for positioning of stars, swirls, crescents, squiggles, and triangles. If your transfers are dark, lighten them with a white eraser until they are just dark enough to see them. It is hard to cover dark transfers with paint.
6. Basecoat designs with light mustard, using a small liner or a round brush. Add some dots and tiny stars around the larger designs. Let dry.
7. Using a 1" flat brush, paint light mustard checks approximately 3/4" apart around rim of frame.
8. Go over the light mustard designs and checks with touches of metallic gold to give a richer look.
9. Finish with several coats of matte varnish. ❑

Pattern for Magical Stripes

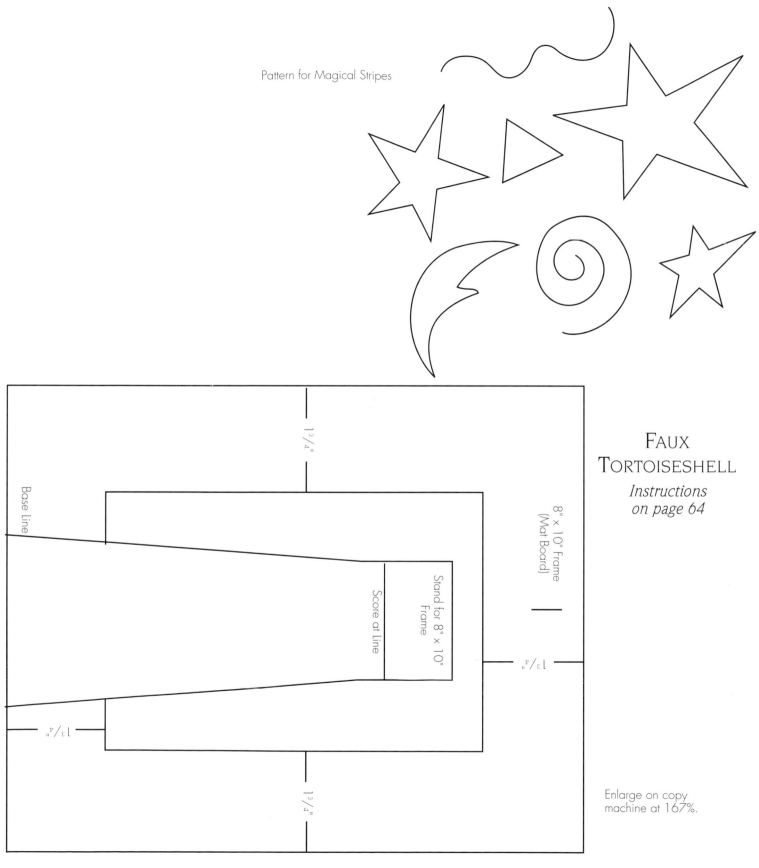

FAUX
TORTOISESHELL

*Instructions
on page 64*

8" x 10" Frame
(Mat Board)

1 3/4"

1 3/4"

1 3/4"

1 3/4"

Base Line

Score at Line

Stand for 8" x 10"
Frame

Enlarge on copy
machine at 167%.

Faux Tortoiseshell
Designed by Patty Cox

■ Materials

Metallic Liquid Leaf Paint:
Gold

Transparent Glass Paint:
Amber
Orange
Yellow

Acrylic Craft Paint:
Black
Burnt umber

Frame Materials:
Mat board, 8" x 10" with 4-3/4" x 6-3/4" opening
Foam core board, 8" x 10" piece plus enough for stand (see pattern on page 63)
Three craft sticks

Other Supplies:
Resin finish
Large flat brush
Old paint brush
Black velvet fabric
Thick white glue
Sugar cubes or similar item to hold frame up from work surface
Business card or similar item for leveling resin

■ Instructions

1. Paint white side of mat board with gold leaf paint, using large flat brush. Let dry.
2. Apply generous beads of the glass paint colors on mat board directly from the containers, using mostly amber paint. Swirl the colors together with a brush, covering entire gold surface of mat. Let paint set about 45 minutes.
3. Streak black and burnt umber acrylic paints diagonally across mat board. Stipple over streaks with an old brush. Let dry.
4. Cover work surface with newspaper. Place mat board on sugar cubes or other items to create a raised level surface. Mix resin finish according to manufacturer's instructions. Spread mixture over the painted mat board with an old business card or similar item. Breathe with short, puffy breaths (whisper "ha ha") over surface to remove any air bubbles. Let dry.
5. Cover an 8" x 10" piece of foam core board with black velvet; miter corners. Use thick white glue to secure. Using pattern of stand, cut a stand from foam core board. Cover it with velvet.
6. Glue craft sticks near sides and bottom of opening on back of frame front as a photo guide.
7. Glue frame front to foam core board backing. Glue stand above scored line to foam core board backing. ❏

Marble & Old Wood
Designed by Kathi Malarchuk

▣ Materials

Acrylic Craft Paint:
Black
Cobalt blue
Dark Green
Ivory
Medium Green

Frame:
Wood frame, 10-1/2" x 12-1/2" x 5/8" thick,
 with 7" x 9" opening
Mat to fit rabbet measurements of frame with 4" x 6" opening

Other Supplies:
Crackle medium
Glazing Medium
Cellulose sponge
Sponge brushes
Feather
Matte acrylic spray sealer

▣ Instructions

Crackled Frame:
1. Basecoat frame with two coats of dark green. Let dry after each coat.
2. Apply crackle medium, following manufacturer's instructions. Let dry.
3. Apply a topcoat of ivory. Cracks will form as topcoat dries. Let dry.
4. Spray with matte acrylic sealer.

Marbleized Mat:
1. Basecoat mat with two coats of dark green. Let dry after each coat.
2. In separate disposable plates for each color, mix some medium green, cobalt blue, black, and ivory with the glazing medium to thin the paint slightly.
3. Dampen cellulose sponge. Dip it into a small amount of medium green and then cobalt blue.
4. Lightly sponge mat with this mixture of color in diagonal drifts. Wipe sponge — do not wash.
5. Repeat sponging with black, then with ivory. Sponge with just a little dark green to add depth.
6. Dip tip of feather into the thinned ivory. Add veins by pulling tip of feather irregularly in diagonal lines that follow diagonal directions of drifts. Let dry.
7. Spray with matte acrylic sealer. ❑

GILDED FRAMES

Whether you have an old frame you wish to rejuvenate or frame you made yourself, there are several products and techniques for giving it a rich metallic finish.

Beautiful gold leaf is one way. This product also comes in a variegated gold type for color interest. Another way is to use a rub-on metallic wax that you apply with your fingers and buff with a soft cloth to a lovely glow. It comes in a variety of metallic colors.

And, of course, there's always paint — this time with a metallic look. One of the interesting frames here is a cardboard frame covered with embossed wallpaper, then given an antiqued bronze finish with paint.

Add the special shine of metal to your frames in your favorite way.

Leaf of Many Colors

Designed by Marie Le Fevre

▨ Materials

Leafing:
Variegated Gold Leaf

Frame:
Any frame you wish to recycle

Other Supplies:
Adhesive sizing for gold leaf
Two utility brushes
Soft cloth or old stocking
Optional: Satin varnish

▨ Instructions

1. Clean frame with mild soap and water to be sure it is free from dust and dirt. Dry with a paper towel.
2. Slightly sand frame.
3. Apply a uniform coat of adhesive sizing with a utility brush. Be sure to cover frame completely. Do not leave any puddles. Wash brush with warm soapy water immediately after use and dry it with a paper towel. Let adhesive dry. As it dries, it will change from a milky white to a transparent clear. This will take about an hour. You can speed the process by using a hair dryer. The adhesive sizing will remain tacky but appear clear.
4. With clean dry hands, pick up a sheet of variegated leaf and apply it to the sticky adhesive surface. Overlap the leaf slightly as you add more pieces to cover the surface. The leaf will stick only to the sticky surface and not to previously applied leaf. When the surface is completely covered, gently smooth the surface with a clean utility brush. Work the leaf into the nooks of the frame. Small cracks and tears may appear on the surface. Pick up small pieces of leaf and apply to those areas if you do not want the color of the frame to show.
5. Use a soft cloth or an old stocking to lightly burnish the leaf.
6. Optional: Apply a uniform coat of varnish over the variegated leaf. Or, you may leave the frame as is without a coat of varnish and the leaf will age and turn dark. ❑

Crackled Gold & Silver

▨ Materials

Acrylic Craft Paint:
Black
Silver metallic

Metallic Finish:
Gold leaf

Frame:
Square wood frame, 5-3/4" x 1/2" thick, with 2-3/4" square opening

Other Supplies:
Adhesive sizing for gold leaf
Two utility brushes
Sponge brushes
Soft cloth or old stocking
Crackle medium

▨ Instructions

1. Basecoat frame with black. Let dry.
2. Brush a heavy coat of crackle medium on front surface of frame with a sponge brush. Refer to manufacturer's directions. Let dry.
3. Brush on a topcoat of silver metallic paint. Cracks will form as topcoat dries. Let dry completely. Also brush the silver topcoat on the rims.
4. Drybrush adhesive sizing in a hit-and-miss or random fashion on front of frame, with a little also on the outside and inside rims. Do not cover entire surfaces. Do not leave any puddles. Wash brush with warm soapy water immediately after use and dry it with a paper towel. Let adhesive dry. As it dries, it will change from a milky white to a transparent clear. This will take about an hour. You can speed the process by using a hair dryer. The adhesive sizing will remain tacky but appear clear.
5. With clean dry hands, pick up a sheet of gold leaf and apply it to the sticky adhesive surface. Overlap the leaf slightly as you add more pieces to cover the areas with adhesive. The leaf will stick only to the sticky surface and not to previously applied leaf. When the adhesive areas are covered, gently smooth the surface with a clean utility brush.
6. Use a soft cloth or an old stocking to lightly burnish the gold leaf. ❑

Gilded Oval
Designed by Marie Le Fevre

■ Materials

Metallic Rub-On Wax:
Gold
Silver
Copper

Frame:
Recycled frame (frame shown is 10-1/2" x 12-1/2" oval with 6-1/4" x 8-1/4" opening)

Other Supplies:
Soft T-shirt cloth

■ Instructions

1. Place a small amount of metallic wax on your finger. Rub the finish evenly but thinly over the surface of the frame. Usually one application is sufficient, but several thin coats may be applied. You may also apply several different colors for a variegated appearance. The frame shown is finished with gold and silver plus a touch of copper metallic waxes. If desired, you can apply the metallic wax with a soft T-shirt cloth. If your frame has a lot of detail, you can apply the metallic wax with a soft brush in order to work the wax into the crevices of the frame.
2. Allow to dry for 30 minutes.
3. Buff with a soft cloth until you have produced a beautiful metallic glow. ❏

Bronzed Flowers

Designed by Kathi Malarchuk

Materials

Acrylic Craft Paint:
Antique bronze metallic
Black
Bronze metallic
Raw umber

Frame:
Corrugated cardboard frame (or three layers of corrugated cardboard cut to 9-1/4" square with 3" square opening stacked and glued together with thick white glue for a 1/2" thick frame)

Other Supplies:
Embossed wallpaper
Craft knife
Masking tape
Sponge brushes
Soft cloth
Matte acrylic spray sealer

Instructions

1. Apply masking tape to inner rim of frame (in opening) and cut off excess.
2. Basecoat frame with one coat of black to prime surface for wallpaper. Let dry.
3. Lay frame on wallpaper. Cut out a piece of wallpaper 1" larger than frame on all sides. Place frame on more wallpaper. Cut out another piece the size of frame.
4. Lay frame on each piece (centered on the larger piece) and mark frame opening. Cut opening from both pieces of wallpaper with craft knife.
5. Prepare and apply larger wallpaper piece to frame following manufacturer's instructions. Align opening of wallpaper with opening of frame. Fold excess paper around outer rims of frame and onto backside. Let dry. Repeat on backside of frame with the smaller wallpaper piece, this time

aligning both the opening and the edges. Let dry.
6. Basecoat wallpaper with raw umber. Let dry for ten minutes and wipe with a soft cloth to remove some of the paint.
7. With sponge brush, add black to selected areas of paper to give depth to color. Wipe with a soft cloth.
8. Pour a small amount of antique bronze paint onto palette. Dip soft cloth into paint and lightly wipe onto raised sections of wallpaper. Repeat with bronze paint.
9. Add black as needed with a soft cloth to create additional depth. Let dry.
10. Spray with matte acrylic sealer. ❏

DECORATING FRAMES
WITH TIN & WIRE

Would you believe it?! Embossed metal frames made from soft drink cans!
A triple frame made from metal outlet covers! Heavy wire bent and coiled into
interesting shapes to decorate a ceramic tile frame! Stars cut from copper!
All these make wonderful, unique frames.
The following pages will tell you how.

Embossed Aluminum Frame
Designed by Patty Cox

▪ Materials

Frame Materials:
Four aluminum soft drink cans (12 oz.)
Two frame mats, 5" x 7", with 3-1/4" x 4-1/4" openings (ready-cut or cut your own according to the pattern from mat board)
Cardboard, a 5" x 7" piece and a 2" x 6" piece for backing

Other Supplies:
Old scissors
Ballpoint pen
Felt
Masking tape
Industrial strength adhesive

Fig. 1

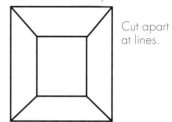

▪ Instructions

Wear protective gloves when cutting or handling metal.

1. Cut away the top and bottom from each 12 oz. aluminum can using old scissors. Cut can open on side (Fig. 1). Rinse and dry aluminum sheets from cans. Trim away jagged edges, leaving aluminum pieces roughly 3-1/2" x 8".

2. Have two frame mats ready or cut two of your own using pattern from matboard. Using frame pattern, rule straight lines on just ONE mat frame from inside corners to outside corners. Cut apart on corner lines. See Fig. 2

3. Place felt on work surface. Lay aluminum sheet, printed side up, on felt. Place one section of mat in center of aluminum. Using a ballpoint pen, firmly draw a line along each side of mat section (Fig. 3). Mark margins on aluminum 3/8" outside scored lines (Fig. 4). Cut out aluminum piece around margins (the shape shown in Fig. 4). Repeat with each mat section and each aluminum sheet.

4. Place a section of aluminum on felt, printed side up. Using the ballpoint pen, firmly draw stars, spirals, zigzags, and double lines on each section according to design pattern. Repeat with each aluminum section.

5. Wrap margins of each embossed aluminum section around its corresponding mat section. Secure aluminum margins on back with masking tape.

6. Glue backsides of aluminum sections onto second mat frame, aligning mitered corners. Lay flat and place a large book on top until glue dries.

7. Cut a 5" x 7" piece of cardboard for frame back. Using stand pattern, cut a frame stand from cardboard.

8. Glue frame back to backside of frame around sides and bottom. Leave top open for inserting photo. Glue frame stand above scored line on frame back. ❏

Patterns for frame and embossing design are on page 74.

Fig. 2 – Mat board frame pieces

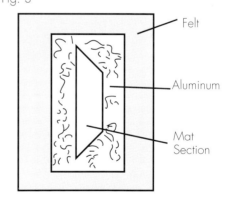

Cut apart at lines.

Fig. 3

Felt

Aluminum

Mat Section

Fig. 4

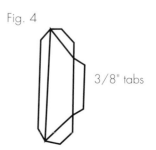

3/8" tabs

Embossed Aluminum Frame
Instructions on page 73

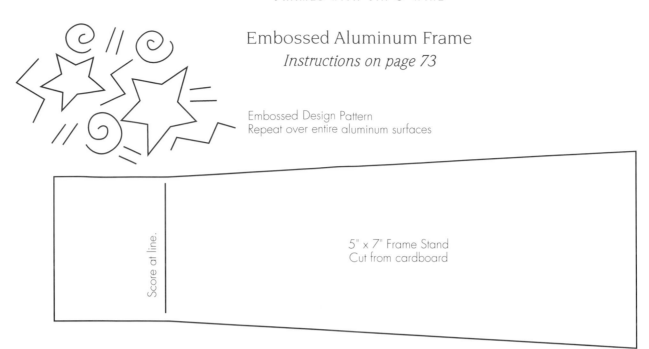

Embossed Design Pattern
Repeat over entire aluminum surfaces

Score at line.

5" x 7" Frame Stand
Cut from cardboard

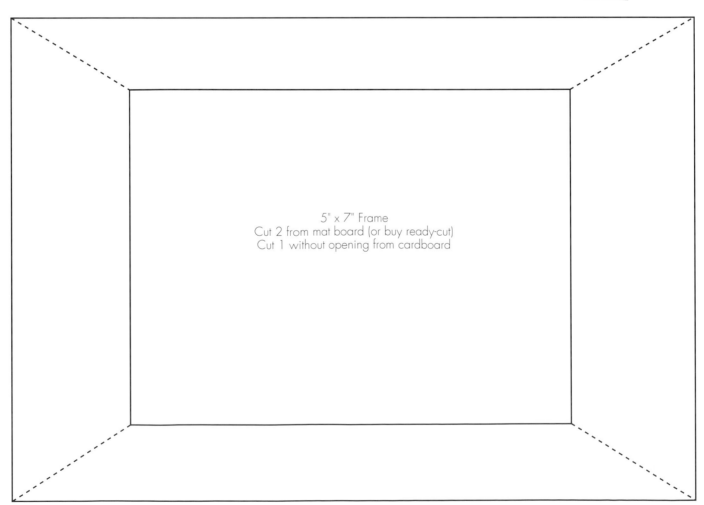

5" x 7" Frame
Cut 2 from mat board (or buy ready-cut)
Cut 1 without opening from cardboard

Copper Coils

Designed by Patty Cox

Materials

Frame Materials:

Tile (green glazed shown), 5-3/4" square
Clear acrylic frame, 3-1/2" square
Precut roof flashing tin, 4-1/2" x 7"

Other Supplies:

One yd. 13-gauge copper wire
Copper sheet (available at hardware stores or check "sheet metal" in Yellow Pages)
Aluminum soft drink can
Needlenose pliers
Hole punch
Old scissors
Household bond cement
Industrial strength adhesive

Instructions

Wear protective gloves when cutting or handling sharp metal.

1. Glue acrylic frame in the center of the tile with adhesive.
2. Cut a 23" length of copper wire. Following pattern, form a coil on each end of wire with coils facing each other. Use needlenose pliers. Make a 90-degree bend in center of this wire as pattern shows. Coil one end of remaining piece of wire as shown in pattern. Glue coils onto tile around acrylic

frame with household cement as shown in Fig. 1.
3. Following patterns, cut three stars from copper sheet with old scissors.
4. Cut the top and bottom from an aluminum soft drink can and discard. From remaining aluminum section, punch six dots with a hole punch.
5. Glue stars and dots on tile with household cement. Refer to photo of project for placement.
6. Bend flashing tin over a straight edge such as a craft stick, 2" from one end. Glue large end of flashing tin to back of tile with adhesive to form a stand. ❑

Fig. 1

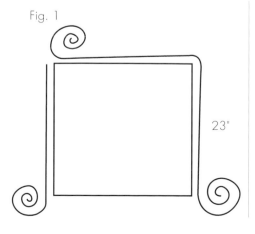

23"

See page 76 for frame pattern.

Copper Coils
Instructions on page 75

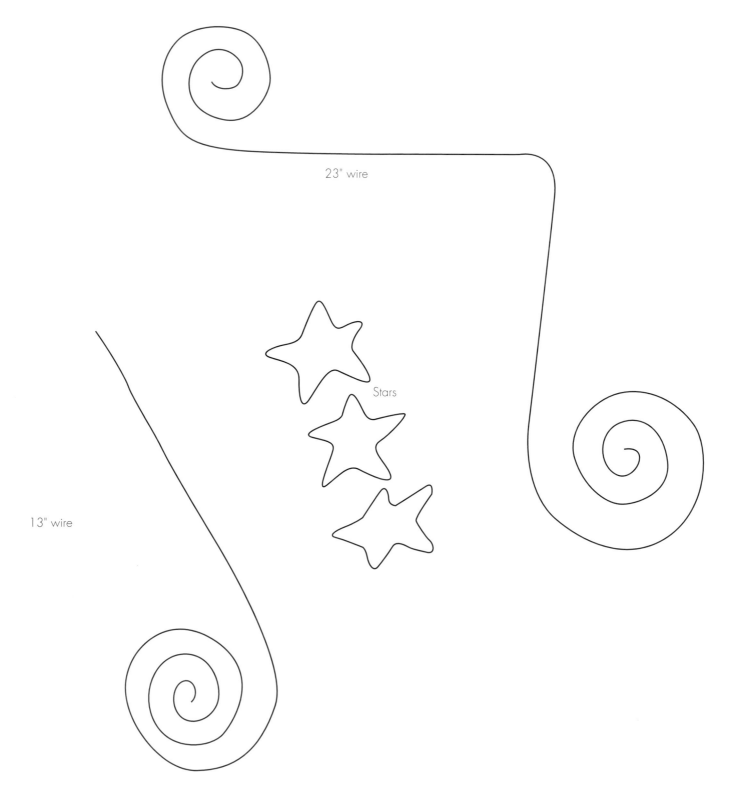

23" wire

Stars

13" wire

Heart Collage Paper Frame
Instructions on page 78

Frame Back (Without Opening)
Cut 1 – Black Foam Core Board

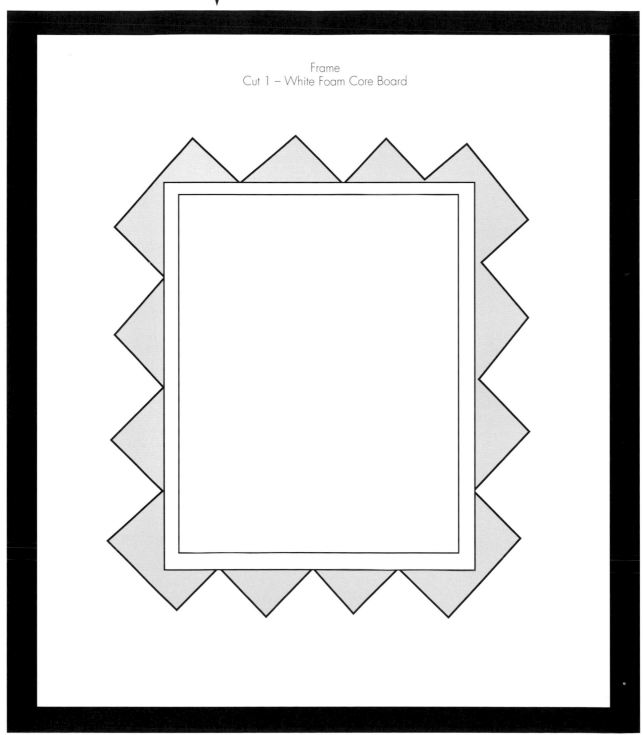

Frame
Cut 1 – White Foam Core Board

Heart Collage Paper Frame
Designed by Patty Cox

▧ Materials

Frame Materials:
White foam core board, 6" x 7"
Black foam core board: one 7-1/2" x 6-1/2" piece; one 2-5/8" x 5-1/4" piece

Other Supplies:
Handmade paper: lime, blue, red, purple
Gold 20-ga wire
Gold thread
Acetate
Three craft stocks
Masking tape
Craft knife
Round nose pliers
Needle
Pinking shears
Thick white glue

Fig. 1

Bend outer end of coil.

Fig. 2
Glue craft sticks on backside of frame to guide pictures squarely into frame.

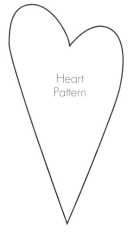

Heart Pattern

Score at Line

Frame Stand
Cut 1
Black Foam Core Board

▧ Instructions

1. Using pattern on page 77, cut frame from white foam core board with a craft knife. Cut frame back (frame pattern without an opening) from black foam core board. Using pattern, cut frame stand from black foam core board.
2. Trace around frame front on lime paper. Cut out 3/4" larger than frame on all sides. Cut an X inside frame opening diagonally from corner to corner of opening.
3. Spread thick white glue evenly over surface of frame. Adhere lime paper to frame. Fold tabs formed by X inside opening to backside, cut excess off margins at outer edges of frame, and tape in place. Fold excess on outer edges to backside and tape in place.
4. Using pattern, cut zigzag border from blue paper with a craft knife. Glue border around center opening on front of frame.
5. Using heart pattern, cut three hearts from red paper. Cut three triangles from purple paper. Glue triangles in place on frame with hearts offset on top of triangles. Refer to photo of project.
6. Cut scraps of black foam core board into small triangles using pinking shears. Glue in place on frame front, as shown in photo.
7. Coil three 4" lengths of 20-gauge gold wire around a pencil. Use round nose pliers to tighten center of coil. Loosen outside of coil by hand. Make a 90-degree bend in outer end of coil as shown in Fig. 1. Stick "stem" of each coil into frame. Dot glue under each coil with a toothpick. Hold coils in position with clothespins until dry.
8. Thread needle with gold thread. Sew through foam core board around hearts. Cover thread ends with masking tape on backside. Stitch small x's over black triangles and here and there on lime background.
9. Cut acetate 1/4" smaller on all sides than frame. Glue acetate on backside of frame.
10. Glue craft sticks on backside of frame to hold picture squarely. See Fig. 2.
11. Glue frame to frame back (cut from black foam core board). Glue frame stand above scored line to backside of frame back. ❑

See page 77 for frame pattern

Outlets For Love
Designed by Patty Cox

■ Materials

Acrylic Craft Paint: Copper metallic

Frame Materials:
Black foam core board, 5-3/8" x 10-1/4"
Three metal single outlet covers with screws
Six metal nuts to fit screws or 1/2" aluminum squares cut from
   soft drink can

Other Supplies:
Copper 13-gauge wire
Sponge
Craft knife
Needlenose pliers
Picture hanger
Craft bond metal & plastic cement
Industrial strength adhesive
Transparent tape or glue stick

■ Instructions

1. Cut a 5-3/8" x 10-1/4" piece of black foam core board.
   Round the corners.
2. Sponge edges of front surface and rims with copper paint.
   Let dry.
3. Arrange outlet covers in position on front of frame as shown
   in photo of project. Stick a needle or long pin through screw
   holes into foam core board to hold outlets in place temporari-
   ly. Position photos on foam core board behind round openings in outlet covers. Tape photos in place or secure them
   with a glue stick.
4. Realign outlet covers. Secure with screws into foam core
   board. Screws will slightly exit the backside of foam core
   board. Screw a nut on the end of each screw or cut a 1/2"
   square from an aluminum can for each screw (six squares);
   punch a nail hole in the center of each, and screw the aluminum squares over ends of screws.
5. Shape three copper wire hearts with needlenose pliers as
   shown by patterns. Glue these on outlet covers with metal-
   and-plastic cement.
6. Glue picture hanger to center top of backside with adhesive.
   ❏

Patterns for Wire Hearts

DECOUPAGED FRAMES

With decoupage, a frame can be tailor-made to commemorate an event such as a wedding or anniversary celebration by decoupaging parts of an invitation or napkin onto it. Frames can be made to suit a special occasion such as Christmas or a special person by decoupaging suitable motifs from greeting cards or giftwrap paper. You can find and use theme motifs from a variety of sources, even magazines and catalogs. And, for a nature theme, even real leaves or twigs can be decoupaged. For dimension, buttons and charms can be included in your designs.

Modern decoupage is very easy, not like the old days of adding layer after layer of finish. Current decoupage finishes require only two or three coats.

Make the frames shown here or alter these ideas to fit the occasions and people in your own life.

Decoupage Supplies You Will Need

Frame: Most any frame can be decoupaged, but the less intricate your molding, the easier and sometimes more successful your project will be. Frames cut of matboard or cardboard are disguised when decoupaged.

Prints: Prints can be obtained from a variety of sources. There are decoupage papers available at craft shops which contain prints made for this purpose. Other sources are art prints, giftwrap paper, greeting cards, postcards, calendars, magazine and catalog prints, photographs, and photocopies of any of these. When the paper is thick, such as on a greeting card, postcard, or photograph, it is best to either photocopy it for a thinner print or separate the plies of the paper for a thinner print. Even items such as leaves and ferns can be decoupaged to a project.

Decoupage Finish: Decoupage finish is a varnish/sealer/glue that simplifies the decoupage process considerably. Use it to adhere your print. Then use it to coat your print and add a finish to the entire piece.

Sponge brush or 1" soft flat brush for applying decoupage finish

Small sharp scissors such as embroidery or cuticle scissors for cutting out printed motifs ❏

Fisherman's Delight

Designed by Patty Cox

■ *Materials*

Acrylic Craft Paint:
Burnt red-orange
Ivory
Red
White

Frame Materials:
Hunter green mat board, 8" x 10"
Tan mat, 5" x 7" with 3-1/4" x 4-1/4"
   opening

Four 12" cinnamon sticks
Raffia
Black foam core board, 8-1/2" x 11"

Other Supplies:
Fishing theme giftwrap paper
Antique decoupage finish
Crackle medium
Twig, 7-1/2" long
Leather thong, scrap, or shoelace
Gold 24-gauge wire, 24" long

Two fishing lures
Round wooden bead, 3/8" diam.
Three craft sticks
Hanging tab or frame stand
Flat paint brush, size 3/4"
Toothpick
Craft knife
Clip clothespins
Large rubber bands
Industrial strength adhesive
Continued on page 84

Fisherman's Delight
Pictured on page 83

continued from page 82

▌Instructions

1. Cut out motifs from giftwrap paper.
2. Apply decoupage finish to hunter green mat board. Arrange and place motifs on mat board. Press motifs with fingers to secure and remove air bubbles. Brush decoupage finish on top of motifs.
3. Paint tan mat with ivory paint. Let dry. Apply a generous coat of crackle medium on top of basecoat. Let dry. Brush on burnt red-orange topcoat. Cracks will form as paint dries.
4. Glue crackled mat in center of decoupaged mat board.
5. Cut two cinnamon sticks to 9-1/2" long by scoring with a craft knife, then snapping off ends. Glue 12" sticks over 9-1/2" sticks, creating a rectangle. Tie each corner with raffia as shown in photo of project. Glue cinnamon stick frame on edges of decoupaged mat board. Secure with clip clothespins and large rubber bands until dry.
6. BOBBER: Paint the 3/8" round bead with white. Let dry. Break off the end of a toothpick and dip toothpick in red paint. Let dry. Glue red toothpick in center opening of bead. Paint top of bead with red.
7. FISHING POLE: Wrap the gold wire in a spiral around a pencil. Remove. Wrap one end of wire around the end of the 7-1/2" twig. Wrap and glue leather thong, a leather scrap, or shoelace on top of wire. Glue the other end of wire into top of bobber. Glue the twig on an angle across upper left corner of frame. Refer to photo of project for positioning.
8. Glue two fishing lures on decoupaged mat board outside of crackled mat.
9. Glue three craft sticks on back of frame opening (on sides and bottom) as a guide for photo.
10. Glue 8-1/2" x 11" piece of black foam core board backing to backside of mat board.
11. Glue a hanging tab on frame stand on frame back. ❏

Yesteryear Christmas
Designed by Kathi Malarchuk

▌Materials

Acrylic Craft Paint:
Medium green

Frame:
Wood frame, 11-1/4" x 12-3/4" with 4-1/2" x 6-1/2" opening

Other Supplies:
Gold foil
Foil adhesive
Various Christmas cards with old fashioned Christmas motifs
Decoupage finish
Small sharp scissors
Sponge brushes
Sm. piece kitchen plastic wrap

▌Instructions

1. Basecoat frame with two coats of medium green. Let dry and sand between coats. Let dry.
2. Apply foil adhesive to front and rims of frame with a crumpled piece of plastic wrap. Let this dry for approximately 30 minutes. Apply foil to frame; it will adhere wherever there is adhesive. Follow manufacturer's instructions.
3. Cut out Christmas motifs from Christmas cards. Brush decoupage finish on backside with a sponge brush. Arrange motifs and adhere them to front of frame. Apply two coats of decoupage finish to entire frame (including on tops of motifs) with a sponge brush. ❏

Fifty Happy Years

Designed by Kathi Malarchuk

Materials

Acrylic Craft Paint: Ivory

Frame:
Wood frame, 11-1/4" x 12-3/4" with 4-1/2" x 6-1/2" opening

Other Supplies:
50th Anniversary greeting cards with appropriate motifs
Decoupage finish
Small sharp scissors; Sponge brushes

Instructions

1. Basecoat frame with two coats of ivory paint. Let dry and sand between coats. Let dry.
2. Cut out sayings, scenes, flowers and other motifs from cards. Brush decoupage finish on backside with a sponge brush. Arrange motifs and adhere them to front of frame. Apply two coats of decoupage finish to entire frame (including on tops of motifs) with a sponge brush. ❑

PERSONALIZED FRAMES

Frames are meant for pictures, but words can be part of the design, as well.
Make a frame for your cat's photo and include his name in the design. Personalize
a frame for a friend with her name on the frame. Even write whole messages to express love or
friendship to create a frame for a special purpose and special person. There are a variety of products that can easily add the words — stencil crayons, painter's pens, or even chalk. You can also
stamp special words in a decorative design with rubber stamps you can find at craft shops.
After all, what is more special than someone's name or the word LOVE?

Personalize Your Painted Frames With a Variety of Products

Stencil Paint Crayons: A stencil paint crayon is an easy product to use for writing a personalization on your painted frame.
Stencil crayons are available in many colors. This avoids the use
of a brush. Allow to dry overnight, then coat with a spray sealer.

Painter's Pens: Messages and personalization can be written
with painter's pens. They are available in a variety of colors and
with different size tips.

Chalk: Write your message or personalization on your painted
frame with chalk. It is available in a variety of colors. To make
it permanent, spray the frame after chalking with matte acrylic
sealer. If you wish to make a frame on which the message can
be changed, spray it *before* chalking with two coats of matte

acrylic sealer; let dry after each coat. Then add chalked lettering. The chalk can be wiped off when desired with a damp
sponge and the frame can be re-chalked.

Rubber Stamps: There are a number of rubber stamps of
words in a decorative design — commonly used "message
words" like LOVE, JOY, FRIEND, and more. These can be used
within your message for an extra design element. Brush ink or
paint on the stamp and press the stamp in place on your project.

On "My True Love" frame, the word love in decorative lettering is stamped on with black ink. When dry, the letters and
flowers around the letters are colored in with diluted paint and
a paint brush. ❏

Blackboard Frame

Designed by Kathi Malarchuk

▓ Materials

Acrylic Craft Paint:
Black
Red-brown

Stencil Paint Crayon:
Light green

Frame:
Corrugated cardboard, 9-1/4" square x
1/2" thick with 3" square opening (if
necessary, glue three pieces of cardboard together for thickness)

Other Supplies:
Sponge brush
Craft knife
Masking tape, 1" wide
Matte acrylic spray sealer

▓ Instructions

1. Cover edges of cardboard frame and
opening with masking tape. At opening,
align one edge of tape with front edge.
Trim off excess tape even with back
edge of rim, using a craft knife. For
outer edge, align one edge of tape with
back edge of frame. Fold excess tape
onto front surface of frame to create

border. Do this for one side of frame at
a time.
2. Basecoat front of frame, inside of the
border with black. Basecoat entire backside with black. Let dry.
3. Basecoat the tape border (including
outer rims of frame) with red-brown.
Let dry.
4. Write lettering ("Razputin [or your cat's
name] the best cat") and draw whiskers
on black area of frame with light green
stencil paint crayon. Refer to photo of
project. Let dry.
5. Spray with matte acrylic sealer. ❏

Greatest Dog Frame

Designed by Kathi Malarchuk

■ Materials

Acrylic Craft Paint:

Aqua   Yellow

Hot pink   White

Frame:

Corrugated cardboard, 9-1/4" square x

1/2" thick with 3" square opening (if necessary, glue three pieces of cardboard together for thickness)

Other Supplies:

Aqua chalk

Palette

Sponge brush

Toothbrush or spattering tool

Craft knife

Masking tape

Matte acrylic spray varnish

continued on page 88

Greatest Dog Frame
Pictured on page 87

continued from page 87

■ Instructions

1. Cover edges of cardboard frame with masking tape. Trim off tape at front and back edges of frame so no tape goes onto front or back surface.
2. Basecoat entire frame with two coats of yellow. Let dry after each coat.
3. Dilute aqua, hot pink, and white paints with water to the consistency of ink. Spatter with each color one at a time over entire frame. Let dry.
4. Write lettering ("Ashley [or your girl friend's name] the greatest girl (or boy) ever") with aqua chalk. Refer to photo of project.
5. Spray with matte acrylic varnish.

Option: If you want to make a frame on which you can change the message, spray with two coats of varnish and let dry before writing message. Then write message. To change message, wipe off chalk with a damp sponge. ❏

My True Love
Designed by Kathi Malarchuk

■ Materials

Acrylic Craft Paint:

Aqua	Light green	Ivory
Blue	Red-brown	Yellow
Brown	Purple	

Frame:

Corrugated cardboard, 9-1/4" square x 1/2" thick with 3" square opening (if necessary, glue three pieces of cardboard together for thickness)

Other Supplies:

"LOVE" stamp; Black ink pad
Black medium tip permanent marker
Paint brush: #0 liner
Sponge brush; Sea sponge
Chalk pencil and ruler
Masking tape; Craft knife
Palette or disposable plate
Matte acrylic sealer

■ Instructions

1. Cover edges of cardboard frame with masking tape. Trim off tape at front and back edges of frame so no tape goes onto front or back surface.
2. Basecoat frame with two coats of ivory. Let dry between coats.
3. With dampened sea sponge, sponge surface lightly with brown. (Dip sponge in paint, dab on palette a time or two to remove excess, then dab sponge on project surface.)
4. Measure and mark spacing for lettering on frame front, leaving spaces for the LOVE stamp after the word "true" and before the word "forever":
   You are my true (STAMP)
   my heart and
   soul, my reason for
   being, the only one
   who will have my (STAMP)
   forever and ever
5. Brush black ink on stamp. Stamp LOVE. Let dry.
6. Write remainder of lettering with the permanent black marker.
7. Dilute acrylic paints to ink consistency. Paint flowers and letters in LOVE, using a liner brush. Let dry.
8. Spray lightly with matte acrylic sealer. ❏

Friends Frame

Designed by Kathi Malarchuk

Materials

Acrylic Craft Paint:
Blue-green
White

Painter's Pens:
Metallic gold, fine point
White, medium and fine points

Frame:
Corrugated cardboard, 9-1/4" square x 1/2" thick with 3" square opening (if necessary, glue three pieces of cardboard together for thickness)

Other Supplies:
Sponge brush
Masking tape, 1" wide
Craft knife
Pencil and ruler
Matte acrylic sealer

Instructions

1. Cover edges of cardboard frame and opening with masking tape. At opening, align one edge of tape with front edge. Trim off excess tape even with back edge of rim, using a craft knife. For outer edge, align one edge of tape with back edge of frame. Fold excess tape onto front surface of frame to create border. Do this for one side of frame at a time.
2. Basecoat front of frame inside border with blue-green. Basecoat entire backside with blue-green. Let dry.
3. Basecoat front border with white. Let dry.
4. Use pencil and ruler to mark spacing for the following message, referring to photo of project. Leave spaces for flowers as shown in photo. Write message with block letters, using the medium white painter's pen for upper case letters and the fine white painter's pen for lower case letters.

FRIENDS are what makes
our LIVES worth living
CHILDHOOD memories of
JOY, of LOVE, of
TEARS and of
SMILES There will always
be DOLLS, and LEMONADE
stands, and PAJAMA parties
to keep our FRIENDSHIP alive

5. Referring to photo, add flowers with the gold painter's pen. Add flower centers with the white painter's pen. Let dry.
6. Spray with matte acrylic sealer. ❏

MIXED MEDIA FRAMES

The following group of frames proves that there is no end to ideas, items, and products that can decorate a frame. Several of these frames are mosaics, created by embedding items in grout such as tiles, and broken china pieces including the intact handles of coffee mugs. Beads and buttons adorn other frames. Mini flower pots, twigs, porcelain roses, and other small, decorative items can give dimension to a frame design, as can real feathers glued onto painted birds. Even old silverware pounded flat is featured on one mixed media design shown here.

So before you discard little bits and pieces, ask yourself, "Could this add beauty to a frame?" ❑

Beads and Silverware

Designed by Patty Cox

▆ Materials

Spray Paint: Chrome

Metallic Rub-On Wax: Gold

Frame:
Clear acrylic box frame, 8-1/2" x 10-1/2"

Other Supplies:
Four old forks
Four old spoons
Faceted round beads, variety of colors:
    6mm, 8mm, and 10mm
Three yds. gold 24-gauge wire
Needlenose pliers
Hammer
Industrial strength adhesive

▆ Instructions

Wear protective gloves and goggles when working with metal.

1. Pound silverware flat on a concrete surface with a hammer.
2. Spray silverware with chrome spray paint. Let dry.
3. Apply gold metallic wax to edges of utensils with your finger.
4. Apply gold metallic wax to edge of top surface and to sides of box frame.
5. Wrap utensils with gold wire, as follows: Cut a 36" length of wire. Fold it in half around the neck of a utensil handle. Criss-cross wires on backside of handle and bring wire to front on both sides. Add a bead. Wrap wires to back and criss-cross them. Bring back to front and add another bead. Continue in this manner until five or six beads are added to each handle.
6. Wrap the tines of two forks and the bowl of two spoons with 18" lengths of wire in an irregular pattern. Add a bead to each as you wrap them.
7. Arrange and glue utensils to frame front as shown in photo of project. Place heavy books on top until glue dries.

Option: Utensils can also be wired to the acrylic frame. Make pinholes in the acrylic frame with a T-pin warmed over a candle flame for 15 seconds. ❑

Beaded Beauty

Designed by Patty Cox

▨ Materials

Spray Paint:
Metallic gold

Frame Materials:
Two mats, 5" x 7" with 3-1/8" x 4-1/4"
   opening
Foam core board: one 5" x 7" piece, one
   2-3/4" x 6" piece

Other Supplies:
One pkg. gold glass rocaille beads, 3.53
   oz. or 100 gram pkg.
15 yds. 28-gauge wire
Masking tape
Old scissors
Craft knife
Needlenose pliers
Three craft sticks
Ribbon, 1" wide x 3" long
Industrial strength adhesive

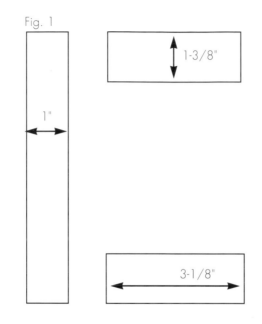

Fig. 1

1-3/8"

1"

3-1/8"

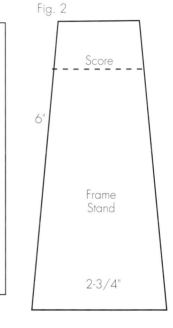

Fig. 2

Score

6"

7"

Frame
Stand

2-3/4"

▨ Instructions

1. Cut one mat apart as shown in Fig. 1, with a craft knife and straight edge. The two sides pieces will measure approximately 1" wide x 7" long. The top and bottom pieces will measure approximately 3-1/8" wide x 1-3/8" deep.
2. Cut approximately one yard of 28-gauge wire. Tape one end of wire to the back of one mat piece. Wrap wire once around end of mat piece.
3. Pour rocaille beans into a cereal bowl. String some beads onto wire, loading enough beads to equal width of mat piece. Bring beads across front of mat and wrap wire around back of mat. Bring wire back to the front and fill with more beads until it is enough to cover front. Bring beads on wire across front for another row of beads. Take wire around back and back to front and continue in this manner. Keep rows of beads close together. When entire front of mat piece is covered with rows of beads, take wire to back and tape in place with masking tape.
4. Repeat step 3 with the other three pieces of the cut mat.
5. Apply adhesive to backside of beaded mat pieces. Position beaded pieces on other mat, aligning them with opening in other mat. Long pieces are on sides and top and bottom pieces are fit between side pieces at top and bottom. Lay flat and place heavy books on top of beaded frame until glue dries.
6. Cut stand from the 2-3/4" x 6" piece of foam core board as shown in Fig. 2. Score across stand 1-1/2" down from top edge (narrow end).
7. Spray paint 5" x 7" foam core frame backing and frame stand with gold metallic paint. Let dry.
8. Glue three craft sticks on backside of frame front near sides and bottom of opening to guide the photo in place.
9. Glue frame front onto foam core frame backing along sides and bottom. Leave top open for inserting photo.
10. Glue frame stand on backside of frame backing. Glue one end of a 3" ribbon to backside of frame stand and the other end to frame, to limit how far frame stand will bend backward. See Fig. 3. ❏

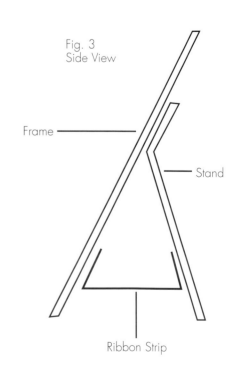

Fig. 3
Side View

Frame

Stand

Ribbon Strip

Mirror & Metal

Designed by Patty Cox

▩ Materials

Frame:
Wood frame, 10-1/2" square with 4-1/2" square opening
Foam core board, 10-1/2" square and 3" x 9" piece
Golden tan leather: 14" square and 7" x 9" piece

Other Supplies:
Twenty 1" square mirrors
Twenty 1-1/4" squares copper sheeting
White grout
Three craft sticks
Disposable glass jar
Bleach
Vinegar
Sponge
Old scissors
Industrial strength adhesive

▩ Instructions

Wear protective gloves when handling or cutting metal.

1. Cut twenty 1-1/4" squares of copper sheeting with old scissors. Place squares in a disposable glass jar. Pour equal parts vinegar and bleach into jar to one-third full or covering all the copper. Lightly shake jar or stir copper to coat all pieces. Allow to oxidize 30 minutes. Remove from mixture. Lay flat until dry.
2. Glue copper and mirror squares on front of wood frame, alternating them in a checkerboard pattern. Let dry.
3. Apply grout around squares according to manufacturer's instructions. Wipe excess away from surface of squares with a sponge.
4. Glue craft sticks to backside of wood frame for a photo guide as shown in Fig. 1.
5. Cover foam core frame back with leather, mitering corners. Cut a frame stand from other piece of foam core board, slanting sides to 2" wide at top. Score across stand 1-1/4" down from top edge. Cover stand with leather. Glue area of stand above scored line on frame back. ❏

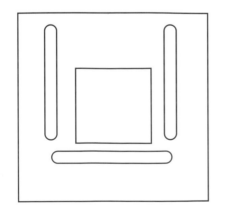

Fig. 1
Craft stick photo guides

Mug Shot

Designed by Patty Cox

◼ Materials

Frame Material:

White foam core board: one 8" x 9" piece with 3-3/4" x 3" opening; one 8" x 9" piece without opening; one 3" x 8" piece

Other Supplies:

Four solid color coffee mugs, different colors

Two pink porcelain rosebuds, approx. 1" diam.

Ten clear glass flat-back marbles

White grout

Bowl of water

Three craft sticks

Dusty rose paper or fabric

Tile nippers

Craft knife

Sponge

Industrial strength adhesive

◼ Instructions

Wear protective gloves and goggles when nipping tiles, breaking china, and applying grout.

1. Cut frame front and back from white foam core board according to the diagram, using a craft knife. To make frame stand, taper long sides of 3" x 8" piece of foam core board to only 2" wide at top. Score across frame stand approximately 1-1/4" down from top edge.

continued on page 96

Mug Shot
Pictured on page 95

continued from page 95

2. Break mugs in an old pillowcase, keeping handles intact.
3. Trim excess rounded ceramic away from mug handles with tile nippers. Arrange and glue handles and porcelain rosebuds on frame front, using a generous amount of adhesive. Allow glue to dry.
4. Arrange and glue clear flat-back marbles on frame front.
5. Nip mug ceramic pieces into 1/2" to 1" pieces. Arrange and glue on frame front. Allow glue to dry.
6. Apply grout with a craft stick or your fingers, being sure to get grout into all crevices. Wipe excess grout off tile and china pieces repeatedly with a wet sponge until ceramics show clearly. Allow grout to set for 15 minutes. Wipe again. Let dry. Polish china and tile pieces with a soft cloth.
7. Cover frame back and stand with dusty pink fabric or paper. Cut these 2" larger all around than frame back and stand. Fold the glue edges around foam core board, mitering corners.
8. Glue three craft sticks on back of frame front near sides and bottom of opening as photo guides.
9. Glue frame front to frame backing, leaving top edge unglued between side craft sticks for inserting photo. Glue frame stand above scored line to backside of frame back. ❏

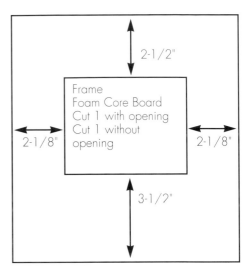

Fig. 1 — Cutting Diagram for frame.

(Frame / Foam Core Board / Cut 1 with opening / Cut 1 without opening)

2-1/2"
2-1/8"
2-1/8"
3-1/2"

Porcelain Rose and Buttons
Designed by Patty Cox

■ Materials

Frame Material:
White foam core board: one 8-1/2" x 6-1/2" piece with 4-3/8" x 2-1/4" opening; one 8-1/2" x 6-1/2" piece with no opening; one 2-3/4" x 5-1/2" piece

Other Supplies:
White grout (This is the product that fills in between ceramic pieces and embeds them. Grout is available at craft shops and home building supply stores.)
Pink porcelain rose, 1-3/4" diam.
Light green tile
Three white embossed china saucers
Assortment of white buttons, approximately 28
Dusty rose paper or fabric
Three craft sticks
Sponge
Bowl of water
Tile nippers (With this tool, you can cut tiles and china pieces to the sizes and shapes you need. They are available at craft shops.)

Craft knife
Industrial strength adhesive (Tiles and china are secured in place on a frame surface with tile adhesive or industrial strength adhesive. Find these at craft shops.)

■ Instructions

Wear protective gloves and goggles when nipping tiles, breaking china, and applying grout.

1. Cut frame front and back from foam core board with a craft knife to dimensions given in materials list. To cut frame stand, taper long sides of the 2-3/4" x 5-1/2" piece of foam core board to just 2" wide at top. Score across frame stand approximately 1-3/8" down from top edge.

continued on next page

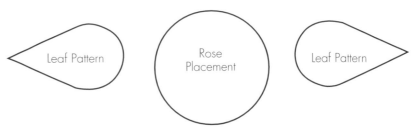

Leaf Pattern

Rose Placement

Leaf Pattern

continued from page 96

2. Using leaf pattern, draw leaves in place on frame front (see photo of frame for positioning).

3. Cut pieces of light green tile with tile nippers. Glue pieces in leaf shapes on frame front. Refer to photo of project. Glue porcelain rose between leaves.

4. Break three white saucers into various size pieces. Arrange and glue on frame front. Let dry.

5. Apply grout with a craft stick or your fingers, being sure to get grout into all crevices. Wipe excess grout off tile and china pieces repeatedly with a wet sponge until ceramics show clearly. Allow grout to set for 15 minutes. Wipe again.

Let dry. Polish china and tile pieces with a soft cloth.

6. Arrange and glue white buttons in an all-over pattern on frame.

7. Cover frame back and stand with dusty pink fabric or paper. Cut these 2" larger all around than frame back and stand. Fold the glue edges around foam core board, mitering corners.

8. Glue three craft sticks on back of frame front near sides and bottom of opening as photo guides.

9. Glue frame front to frame backing, leaving top edge unglued between side craft sticks for inserting photo. Glue frame stand above scored line to backside of frame back. ❏

Tiled Garden

Designed by Patty Cox

■ Materials

Acrylic Craft Paint:
Teal

Frame Material:
White foam core board: two 7" x 10" pieces and one 3" x 8" piece

Other Supplies:
White tiles
Yellow Tiles
Three orange buttons, 7/8" diam.
Three 1/2" squares of white foam core board
Terra cotta colored grout
Five terra cotta flower pots, 1-1/4" tall
Green moss or lichen
Pkg. 3/16" turquoise plastic beads
Three craft sticks
Bowl of water
Sponge
Paint brush
Jewelry glaze
Tile nippers
Industrial strength adhesive
Matte acrylic sealer

■ Instructions

Wear protective gloves and goggles when nipping tiles, breaking china, and applying grout.

1. Cut frame front and back from white foam core board according to the pattern, using a craft knife. To make frame stand, taper long sides of 3" x 8" piece of foam core board to only 2" wide at top. Score across frame stand approximately 1" down from top edge.
2. Draw a pencil line around frame front 3/8" from outer edges.
3. Arrange and glue flower pots on frame. Refer to photo of project.

4. Glue a 1/2" foam core board square to the backside of each orange button. Position and glue buttons on frame.
5. Cut yellow and white tiles into squares approximately 3/8" with tile nippers. Arrange and glue white squares along inside edge of pencil line. Cut squares smaller as needed around pots. Arrange and glue yellow tile pieces bordering opening of frame and inside the white tile outer border. Fill in remaining areas with white tile pieces. Allow glue to dry.
6. Apply grout with a craft stick or your fingers, being sure to get grout into all crevices. Wipe excess grout off tile and china pieces repeatedly with a wet sponge until ceramics show clearly. Allow grout to set for 15 minutes. Wipe again. Let dry. Polish china and tile pieces with a soft cloth.
7. Apply glue along the 3/8" outer edge of frame. Pour turquoise beads into the glue. Let dry. Seal beads with jewelry glaze.
8. Paint frame back, rims of frame front, and frame stand with teal paint. Let dry. Spray with matte acrylic sealer. Let dry.
9. Glue three craft sticks on back of frame front near sides and bottom of opening as photo guides.
10. Glue frame front to frame backing, leaving top edge unglued between side craft sticks for inserting photo. Glue frame stand above scored line to backside of frame back.
11. Glue lichen or moss in terra cotta pots. ❏

Enlarge pattern on copy machine @182%.

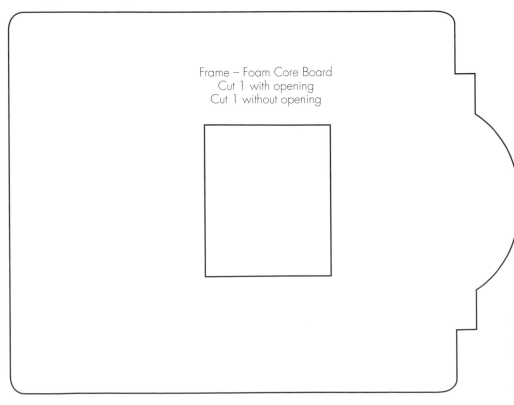

Frame – Foam Core Board
Cut 1 with opening
Cut 1 without opening

Birds of a Feather

Designed by Kathi Malarchuk

▰ Materials

Acrylic Craft Paint:
Light butter-yellow

Acrylic Glazes:
Black
Brown
Ecru
Green
Red-brown

Frame:
Corrugated cardboard, 9-1/4" square x
1/2" thick with 3" square opening (if
necessary, glue three pieces of cardboard together for thickness)

Other Supplies:
Foam stamps of bird and oak leaf
Feathers
Moss
Twigs
Masking tape
Sponge brush
Flat artist's brush
Pencil
Craft knife
Hot glue and glue gun
Matte acrylic sealer

▰ Instructions

1. Cover edges of cardboard frame with masking tape. Trim tape even with edges.
2. Basecoat entire frame with two coats of butter-yellow paint. Let dry after each coat.
3. Brush brown, red-brown, ecru, and black glazes on bird stamp. Refer to photo of project for placement of colors on stamp. Stamp two birds on front of frame as shown in photo of project.
4. Lay twigs on front of frame in the arrangement you like. Lightly mark with pencil where leaves should be placed. Remove twigs.
5. Brush green and red-brown glazes on leaf stamp and stamp leaves where you have marked. Stamp two or three times before reloading stamp for a variety of intensity. Vary the placement of colors each time you reload stamp.
6. Hot-glue twigs and moss to front of frame. Hot-glue feathers to wings of birds.
7. Lightly spray with matte acrylic sealer. ❏

Topiary Garden

Designed by Kathi Malarchuk

▰ Materials

Acrylic Craft Paint:
Light green

Acrylic Glazes:
Dark green
Red-brown

Frame:
Corrugated cardboard, 9-1/4" square x
1/2" thick with 3" square opening (if
necessary, glue three pieces of cardboard together for thickness)

Other Supplies:
Two small clay flower pots broken in half
vertically, 2" tall
Moss
Twigs
Small pebbles
Masking tape
Small sea sponge
Sponge brush
Craft knife
Matte acrylic sealer

▰ Instructions

1. Cover edges of cardboard frame with masking tape. Trim tape even with edges.
2. Basecoat entire frame with two coats of light green paint. Let dry after each coat.
3. Sponge frame with dark green and red-brown, using a damp sea sponge. Let dry.
4. Hot-glue half-pots below and to the sides of frame opening. Refer to photo of project for position. Glue a twig into center of each pot and to frame along sides of opening. Glue pebbles into pots. Shape moss into balls and glue one to top of each twig.
5. Glue twigs to each edge of opening.
6. Spray with matte acrylic sealer. ❏

Pictured right

HANDMADE PAPER & CARDBOARD DECORATIONS

Handmade paper, which can be purchased at craft shops, has a charm of its own. This charm can be imparted to a frame. Cover the frame with the paper or cut out shapes of the paper to adorn the frame. On one frame shown here, the frame is covered with handmade paper on top of heavy swirly lines of dried tube paint for a dimensional design.
Cardboard and heavy art paper are other useful products. Stamp motifs with paint onto art paper, cut out, and glue to the frame. Or use the corrugation made for corrugated cardboard for a textural design.
It's not only beautiful, but inexpensive and easy. ❏

Pictured right: Swirl Relief Frame and Shaped & Textured Frame. Instructions follow.

Swirl Relief
Designed by Patty Cox

Materials

Frame Material:
White foam core board: two 8" x 10" pieces; one 4" x 5-3/4" piece

Other Supplies:
Ecru handmade paper (select a paper without large chunks of pulp)
Dimensional fabric paint, color similar to paper
Three craft sticks
Acetate sheet, 6" x 6-1/2"
Three craft sticks
Masking tape
Craft knife
Thick white glue

Instructions

1. Using pattern on page 104, cut opening from one 8" x 10" piece of foam core board for frame front. Cut frame stand from small piece of foam core board by tapering long sides to 1-1/2" wide at top. Score across frame stand 1-1/2" down from top edge.
2. Transfer swirl pattern to frame front. Using dimensional fabric paint, follow swirl lines, circles, and dots with a generous amount of paint directly from the tube. Allow to dry thoroughly.
3. Cut a piece of handmade paper 2" larger all around than frame front. Wet paper under faucet. Brush a mixture of thick white glue + water on surfaces of frame front. Place wet paper over surface. Press paper over the dimensional paint lines with your fingers, carefully pressing out all air bubbles. Press paper snugly to frame around paint lines because the paper shrinks slightly as it dries.
4. Turn paper edges to backside, mitering corners. Cut an X in paper over frame opening, diagonally from corner to corner of opening. Turn tabs to backside. Let frame dry.
5. Cover frame backing (8" x 10" foam core board without an opening). Use the same technique and miter corners. Cover frame stand with paper in the same manner.
6. Glue and tape acetate in position on back of frame front behind opening. Glue craft sticks around frame opening on backside as a photo guide, as shown in Fig. 1 on page 4.
7. Glue frame front to frame back, leaving an opening on top edge for inserting photo. Glue frame stand above the scored line to back of frame backing above the score line. ❏

Frame pattern and Fig. 1 are on page 104.

Swirl Relief
Instructions on page 102

Enlarge pattern on copy machine @135%.

Swirl Design Pattern

Frame
Foam Core Board
Cut 1 with opening
Cut 1 without opening.

Fig. 1
Craft Stick
Photo Guide

Shaped & Textured

Designed by Patty Cox

Pictured on page 103

■ Materials

Frame:
Acrylic box frame, 5" x 7"

Other Supplies:
Sheet of corrugated cardboard, 12" x 18"
Craft knife
Hole punch
Industrial strength adhesive

■ Instructions

1. Cut frame piece and two side pieces from corrugated cardboard as shown by patterns.
2. Glue curved top and bottom pieces to each long side of acrylic frame, aligning straight edges with back edges of frame. Glue frame end piece to the short side of acrylic frame where 2-1/2" width joins the wide side of top and bottom. Apply glue to curved edges of top and bottom pieces and to front edge of end piece. Place frame front piece over these glued edges, letting excess extend at one short end for now. Apply pressure to surface with lightweight objects until glue dries. Glue remainder of front frame piece to other end of acrylic frame wrapping around to back edge.
3. From remaining corrugated cardboard, cut three 2-part leaves, using leaf pattern and a craft knife. To make cutouts in leaves, start at the wide rounded end of each cutout by punching a hole with a hole punch, then cut the points of the cutouts with a craft knife. This is shown on leaf pattern.
4. Glue leaves on front of frame as shown in photo of project. ❏

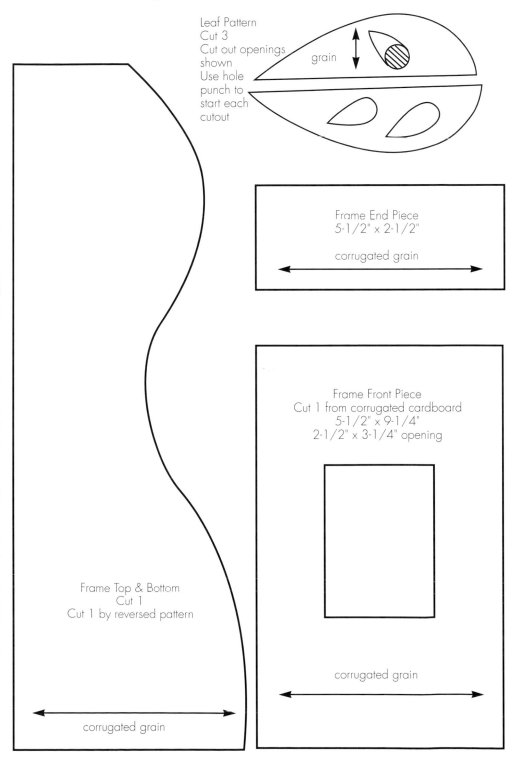

Leaf Pattern
Cut 3
Cut out openings shown
Use hole punch to start each cutout

grain

Frame End Piece
5-1/2" x 2-1/2"

corrugated grain

Frame Front Piece
Cut 1 from corrugated cardboard
5-1/2" x 9-1/4"
2-1/2" x 3-1/4" opening

corrugated grain

Frame Top & Bottom
Cut 1
Cut 1 by reversed pattern

corrugated grain

Antique Letter
Designed by Patty Cox

▨ Materials

Frame:
White foam core board: two 7-3/4"
squares; one 3-1/4" x 5-1/4" piece

Other Supplies:
Ecru handmade paper
Acetate sheet
Gold leaf and leaf adhesive
Black decorating chalk
Envelope sealing wax and stamp or candle
wax and 5/8" button to use as a stamp
Three tiny fern sprigs
Three craft sticks
Cotton swab
Craft knife
Masking tape
Thick white glue

▨ Instructions

1. Using pattern, cut opening from one 7-3/4" square of foam core board, using a craft knife.

2. Trace around frame front on handmade paper, also tracing opening. Cut out paper 3/4" larger all around than marked frame size. Cut an X diagonally from corner to corner of opening.

3. Spread thick white glue evenly over surface of frame front. Adhere paper to frame. Fold tabs in opening to backside and tape in place. Glue excess paper around edges onto backside of frame, mitering corners.

4. If desired, also cover frame backing (the second 7-3/4" square of foam core board) with handmade paper.

5. Tear envelope flap from handmade paper, using pattern. Rub deckled edges with gold leaf adhesive, then apply gold leaf to torn edge. Glue flap to center top of frame front. Turn top edge to backside and tape in place.

6. Using patterns, cut circle and wavy line from acetate for stencils with a craft knife.

7. Rub a cotton swab in black chalk. Place wavy line stencil on frame front. Stencil seven rows of wavy lines with black chalk. Position circle stencil near or on wavy lines and stencil with black chalk, using cotton swab. Refer

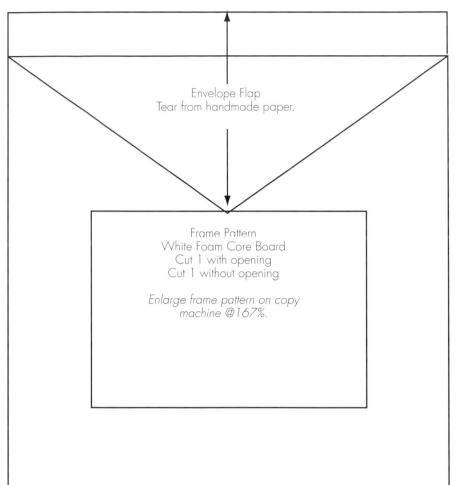

Envelope Flap
Tear from handmade paper.

Frame Pattern
White Foam Core Board
Cut 1 with opening
Cut 1 without opening

Enlarge frame pattern on copy machine @167%.

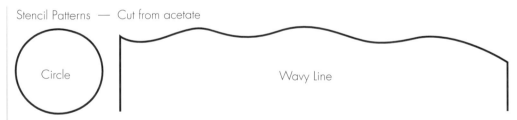

Stencil Patterns — Cut from acetate

Circle

Wavy Line

to photo of project.

8. Glue tiny fern sprigs near point of flap.

9. Make a sealing wax stamp on a piece of acetate. If a sealing wax and a stamp is not available, use candle wax and use a button as a stamp. Lift wax from acetate. Glue it in position over the stems of the fern sprigs.

10. Cut a piece of acetate 1/4" smaller all around than frame front. Glue or tape acetate on backside of frame front.

11. If desired, glue craft sticks on backside of frame front near opening on sides and bottom as a photo guide to hold photo squarely.

12. Glue frame front to frame back, gluing along craft sticks. Leave top open for inserting photo. Glue frame stand above the scored line to backside of frame back. ❏

Abstract Heart

Designed by Patty Cox

■ Materials

Dimensional Paint:
Metallic gold

Frame Materials:
White foam core board
Wire coat hanger

Other Supplies:
Handmade paper, red and purple
Five black flat-back marbles
Acetate sheet
Masking tape
Two craft sticks
Craft knife
Needlenose pliers
Thick white glue

■ Instructions

1. Cut frame front and frame back according to patterns from white foam core board with a craft knife.
2. Glue heart-shaped frame front on red paper. Cut out paper 1" larger all around than heart. Cut an X in the red paper in frame opening diagonally from corner to corner. Fold tabs to backside and tape down. Make cuts in outer margins of paper from edge up to frame every 1/2". Turn tabs around edges to backside and tape.
3. Glue frame back onto purple paper. Cut out paper 1" larger all around than frame back. Turn edges of paper to backside, mitering corners. Cover backside of frame back with purple paper, gluing it in place.
4. Break craft sticks in half. Glue three craft stick pieces to frame back for a photo guide as shown on frame back pattern.
5. FRONT WIRE STAND: Cut away hook from coat hanger. Bend coat hanger as shown in pattern with needlenose pliers.
6. Glue frame front to frame back as shown in photo. Sandwich front wire stand between front and back as shown in photo of project. Leave top unglued for inserting photo.
7. Draw x's on rounded side of black marbles with dimensional paint. Let dry.
8. Glue marbles to frame front as shown in photo of project.
9. BACK WIRE STAND: Shape remaining coat hanger wire into stand back according to the pattern. Cut ends evenly. Bend 1/4" on each end to a 90-degree angle as shown on pattern. Apply glue to the bent 1/4" ends and insert into backside of frame back. ❏

Enlarge patterns on copy machine @200%

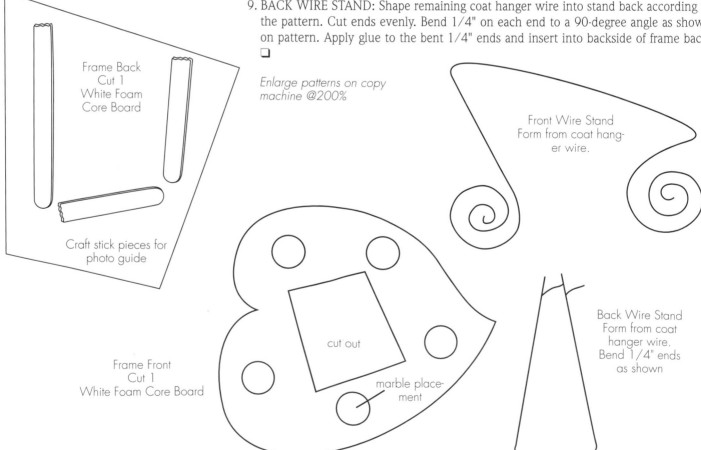

Frame Back
Cut 1
White Foam
Core Board

Craft stick pieces for
photo guide

Front Wire Stand
Form from coat hang-
er wire.

Frame Front
Cut 1
White Foam Core Board

cut out

marble place-
ment

Back Wire Stand
Form from coat
hanger wire.
Bend 1/4" ends
as shown

Honey Bees

▊ Materials

Acrylic Craft Paint:
Paprika color

Frame Material:
Mat board, 15" square

Other Supplies:
Yellow handmade paper, 18" square
Heavy gauge ivory-colored art paper, 8"
    square
Bee design foam stamp, 4" wide
Heavy gauge acetate, 5" square
Sponge wedge applicator or cosmetic wedge
Masking tape
Craft knife
Ruler with metal straight edge
Small sharp scissors (cuticle, embroidery,
    or decoupage)
Pencil
Thick white glue
Mounting adhesive (preferably aerosol)
Disposable plate

▊ Instructions

1. Cut the 15" square of mat board into quarters, resulting in four 7-1/2" mat board squares. Use a craft knife and straight edge. You will use only three of the four pieces.
2. Cut a 4" square opening in the center of one piece for frame front.
3. Cut four 9" square of yellow handmade paper.
4. Coat the front of mat board that has the opening with mounting adhesive. Lay it face down onto center of one yellow paper square. With scissors, cut the yellow paper as shown in Fig. 1. Spread white glue onto the backside of the mat board frame front and wrap the yellow paper margins around to the backside.
5. Score diagonally across one of the remaining mat board squares, using a craft knife and straight edge. See Fig. 1. Do not cut all the way through the piece. Score it just enough so that it can be bent back.

6. Cover the scored mat board square and the other remaining mat board square with yellow paper in the same manner as frame front, except there will be no center opening in these pieces.
7. Also cover the backside of the scored mat board square. Cut the yellow paper for this to the exact size of the mat board square with no margins. Coat backside of the mat board square with mounting adhesive and place yellow paper onto it, aligning edges.
8. Glue the acetate square to the backside of frame front behind the opening. Use masking tape to cover the edges of the acetate and to add more security to the bond.
9. Place the frame front (the square with opening) face down. Squeeze a bead of white glue around only three side edges of this piece as shown in Fig. 3. Place the uncovered side of the unscored mat board onto the glue, aligning edges of the frame front with the second piece of mat board. Squeeze the edges together to bond the glue. With a damp cloth, wipe off any excess glue that squeezes out. The edge that is not glued together will be the top of the frame. You will slide your photo through this edge and into place behind the acetate-covered opening. Place this piece between heavy books until the glue has dried.

Continued on next page

10. Place the frame face down with the open edge at top. Draw a diagonal line from top left corner to bottom right corner on backside of frame. Spread white glue on the top right half as shown in Fig. 4. Place the scored mat board square onto frame piece. Match the scored line with the drawn line of frame. The unglued triangle of the frame backing will be bent back so the frame can stand on its own.

11. Squeeze out paprika-colored paint onto a disposable plate. Dab the sponge applicator or cosmetic wedge into paint. Then dab paint onto stamp design until entire design is coated with a thin layer of paint.

12. Place stamp face down on art paper and press with your hand. Lift to reveal the bee design. Repeat, stamping four bee designs. Let dry.

13. Cut out bee design with small scissors, leaving a 1/16" margin of paper around the design.

14. Glue a bee to each corner of the frame with white glue. Glue only the bee bodies to the frame for a more dimensional effect. ❑

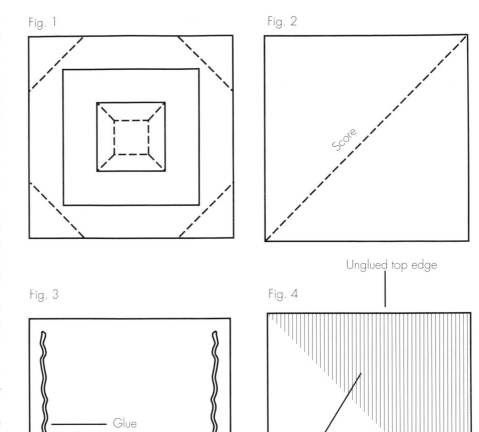

Fig. 1

Fig. 2

Score

Unglued top edge

Fig. 3

Fig. 4

Glue

Spread glue

METRIC CONVERSION CHART

INCHES TO MILLIMETERS AND CENTIMETERS

Inches	MM	CM	Inches	MM	CM	Yards	Meters
1/8	3	.3	4	102	10.2	3/4	.69
1/4	6	.6	5	127	12.7	7/8	.80
3/8	10	1.0	6	152	15.2	1	.91
1/2	13	1.3	7	178	17.8	1-1/2	1.37
5/8	16	1.6	8	203	20.3	1-5/8	1.49
3/4	19	1.9	9	229	22.9	1-3/4	1.60
7/8	22	2.2	10	254	25.4	1-7/8	1.71
1	25	2.5	11	279	27.9	2	1.83
1-1/4	32	3.2	12	305	30.5	2-1/2	2.29
1-1/2	38	3.8				3	2.74
1-3/4	44	4.4	**YARDS TO METERS**			4	3.66
2	51	5.1	Yards	Meters		5	4.57
2-1/2	64	6.4	1/8	.11		6	5.49
3	76	7.6	1/4	.23		7	6.40
3-1/2	89	8.9	3/8	.34		8	7.32
			1/2	.46		9	8.23
			5/8	.57		10	9.14

Index